MIDDLE GRADES MATHEMATICS PROJECT

Spatial Visualization

Mary Jean Winter

Glenda Lappan

Elizabeth Phillips

William Fitzgerald

Addison-Wesley Publishing Company

Menlo Park, California • Reading, Massachusetts • Don Mills, Ontario
Wokingham, England • Amsterdam • Sydney • Singapore
Tokyo • Mexico City • Bogotá • Santiago • San Juan

This book is published by the Addison-Wesley Innovative Division.

The blackline masters in this publication are designed to be used with appropriate duplicating equipment to reproduce copies for classroom use. Addison-Wesley Publishing Company grants permission to classroom teachers to reproduce these masters.

ISBN 0-201-21477-6

13 14 15 - ML - 95 94 93

About the authors

William Fitzgerald, Ph.D. in mathematics education, University of Michigan, joined the faculty of Michigan State University in 1966 and has been Professor of Mathematics and Education since 1971. He has had extensive experience at all levels of mathematics teaching and has been involved in the development of mathematics laboratories.

Glenda Lappan, B.A., Mercer University, Macon, Georgia, and Ed.D., University of Georgia, is Professor of Mathematics at Michigan State University. She directed the mathematics component of MSU Sloan Foundation Minority Engineering Project. She has taught high school mathematics and since 1976 has worked regularly with students and teachers of grades 3–8.

Elizabeth Phillips, B.S. in mathematics and chemistry, Wisconsin State University, and M.S. in mathematics, University of Notre Dame, was visiting scholar in mathematics education at Cambridge University, England. She conducts inservice workshops for teachers and is the author of several papers and books. Currently she is a faculty member in the Department of Mathematics at Michigan State University.

Janet Shroyer, B.S., Knox College, and Ph.D., Michigan State University, has taught mathematics in Lansing public schools and at Oregon College of Education. She was a consultant in the Office of Research Services, evaluator of a teacher corps project, and a research intern in the Institute for Research on Teaching. Presently she is Associate Professor in the Mathematics Department of Aquinas College, Grand Rapids, Michigan.

Mary Jean Winter, A.B., Vassar College, and Ph.D. in mathematics, Carnegie Institute of Technology, has been Professor of Mathematics at Michigan State University since 1965. She has been involved in mathematics education at both school and college (teacher training) level since 1975. She has been especially interested in developing middle school and secondary activities using computers and other manipulatives.

A special note of recognition

Sincere appreciation is expressed to the following persons for their significant contribution to the Middle Grades Mathematics Project.

Assistants:

David Ben-Haim
Alex Friedlander
Zaccheaus Oguntebi
Patricia Yarbrough

Consultant for evaluation:

Richard Shumway

Consultants for development:

Keith Hamann
John Wagner

Contents

Spatial Visualization

The Middle Grades Mathematics Project (MGMP) is a curriculum program developed at Michigan State University funded by the National Science Foundation to develop units of high quality mathematics instruction for grades 5 through 8. Each unit

- is based on a related collection of important mathematical ideas
- provides a carefully sequenced set of activities that leads to an understanding of the mathematical challenges
- helps the teacher foster a problem-solving atmosphere in the classroom
- uses concrete manipulatives where appropriate to help provide the transition from concrete to abstract thinking
- utilizes an instructional model that consists of three phases: launch, explore, and summarize
- provides a carefully developed instructional guide for the teacher
- requires two to three weeks of instructional time

The goal of the MGMP materials is to help students develop a deep, lasting understanding of the mathematical concepts and strategies studied. Rather than attempting to break the curriculum into small bits to be learned in isolation from each other, MGMP materials concentrate on a cluster of important ideas and the relationships that exist among these ideas. Where possible the ideas are embodied in concrete models to assist students in moving from the concrete stage to more abstract reasoning.

THE INSTRUCTIONAL MODEL: LAUNCH, EXPLORE, AND SUMMARIZE

Many of the activities in the MGMP are built around a specific mathematical challenge. The instructional model used in all five units focuses on helping students solve the mathematical challenge. The instruction is divided into three phases.

During the first phase the teacher *launches* the challenge. The launching consists of introducing new concepts, clarifying definitions, reviewing old concepts, and issuing the challenge.

The second phase of instruction is the class *exploration*. During exploration, students work individually or in small groups. Students may be gathering data, sharing ideas, looking for patterns, making conjectures, or developing other types of problem-solving strategies. It is inevitable that students will exhibit variation in progress. The teacher's role during exploration is to move about the classroom, observing individual performances and encouraging on-task behavior. The teacher urges students to persevere in seeking a solution to the

Introduction

challenge. The teacher does this by asking appropriate questions and by providing confirmation and redirection where needed. For the more able students, the teacher provides extra challenges related to the ideas being studied. The extent to which students require attention will vary, as will the nature of attention they need, but the teacher's continued presence and interest in what they are doing is critical.

When most of the students have gathered sufficient data, they return to a whole class mode (often beginning the next day) for the final phase of instruction, *summarizing*. Here the teacher has an opportunity to demonstrate ways to organize data so that patterns and related rules become more obvious. Discussing the strategies used by students helps the teacher to guide them in refining these strategies into efficient, effective problem-solving techniques.

The teacher plays a central role in this instructional model. The teacher provides and motivates the challenge and then joins the students in exploring the problem. The teacher asks appropriate questions, encouraging and redirecting where needed. Finally, through the summary, the teacher helps students to deepen their understanding of both the mathematical ideas involved in the challenge and the strategies used to solve it.

To aid the teacher in using the instructional model, a detailed instructional guide is provided for each activity. The preliminary pages contain a rationale; an overview of the main ideas; goals for the students; and a list of materials and worksheets. Then a script is provided to help the teacher teach each phase of the instructional model. Each page of the script is divided into three columns:

TEACHER ACTION	TEACHER TALK	EXPECTED RESPONSE
This column includes materials used, what to display on the overhead, when to explain a concept, when to ask a question, etc.	This column includes important questions and explanations that are needed to develop understandings and problem-solving skills, etc.	This column includes correct responses as well as frequent incorrect responses and suggestions for handling them.

Worksheet answers, when appropriate, and review problem answers are provided at the end of each unit; and for each unit test, an answer key and a blackline master answer sheet is included.

Introduction

Copyright © 1986 Addison-Wesley Publishing Company, Inc.

RATIONALE

Most students' mathematical experience with the three-dimensional world is obtained from two-dimensional pictures. The use of pictures in place of objects may be difficult, yet it is necessary that students learn to cope with two-dimensional representations of their world. It is important for students to explore pictures or moving pictures on television screens or computer graphics. Students must be able not only to read information from two-dimensional pictures of the real world, but also to represent information about the real world with two-dimensional pictures.

Because of their flexibility and overall usefulness, cubes are used as the basic building blocks for three-dimensional objects. As the students build buildings from the cubes and look at them in different ways, they use their spatial skills in more discriminating ways. They learn visually to distinguish between a left-right or front-back orientation in both two and three dimensions. For example, the picture below shows a left-right orientation in two dimensions.

Learning to visualize the opposite side of an object is a critical step in helping students answer questions on volume, which are found in textbooks and all standardized tests. For example, how many cubes does it take to build the object shown below, or what is its volume? Students may incorrectly answer 10, counting only blocks showing, or 16, counting every *face* showing. Students need experience in building and looking at three-dimensional objects before they can make inferences from two-dimensional drawings.

The enthusiasm, perseverence, and success exhibited by students and teachers while engaged in these activities have convinced us that middle-grade students enjoy working with cubes and that they need the concrete spatial experiences provided by this unit. As one student summed up her experiences, "Now I see giant cubes everywhere!"

Introduction

Three themes—build, draw, and evaluate—are considered in various combinations throughout the unit. Two different schemes for picturing buildings are developed, and the relationships between the two are explored.

In the first scheme, each object is represented by three grid-paper pictures, which are called a set of plans. The first picture is a plan of the base of the building, showing exactly where blocks touch the ground; the second picture is a flat projection viewed from the front; and the third picture is a flat projection viewed from the right side. Note that the method for determining the base plan differs from the way in which the front and right plans are determined.

In order to have formal understanding of this first scheme, a student has to (1) see how a plan and its building are related to each other; (2) be able to draw a plan of an existing building; (3) build a building from a given plan; and (4) be able to construct and represent a building and evaluate the construction of another building. These four steps, in the order given, are the guidelines for the first four activities. In addition, the limitations of this way of representing buildings are explored.

In the first scheme, only one building face is seen at a time. In the second scheme, the building is turned so that three faces of the building can be seen at once. In order to make drawings of these views easier for the students to visualize, isometric dot paper (paper with dots arranged on diagonals rather than rows) is used. The same four steps used in the first scheme serve as guidelines in the second, and similarities and differences between the two schemes are discussed.

In the second scheme students are asked to perform some fairly demanding visualization tasks. They are asked mentally to rotate a building and draw views of the other corners. Cubes are always available to help students who need to see the concrete object in order to be successful.

Students enjoy working with blocks. However, 25 to 30 students in a classroom working with blocks and several different activity sheets call for some general guidelines for management. The following suggestions come from teachers who have taught the unit.

1. Count out all the blocks a student will need and give each student the required number. For all activities 15 blocks packaged in a small plastic bag will suffice. In some activities students need to work together and pool their blocks.

2. Build on old magazines, newspapers, or packs of computer sheets to cut down on noise.

3. Worksheets may be run off back to back to save paper and distribution time. Further time may be saved by handing out all the worksheets for a given activity (with the blocks) at the start of the activity.

4. Homework may be checked by the class. A transparency of the worksheet may be placed on the overhead and the answers written on the transparency (or an overlay). In this way the transparency of the worksheet may be used for giving directions or launching the activity and then for checking the answers or for summarizing.

Introduction

5. Most worksheets may be done at home if students have access to blocks. Some students have younger brothers and sisters with blocks; some have used sugar cubes; and some have been allowed to check blocks out from the school.

6. Standard grading procedures are not so effective in this unit as in others. All students will continue to improve their visualization skills as the unit proceeds. Some teachers have used one of the following: checks (✔) if a worksheet (or activity) was completed or attempted; a combination of plus and minus for each worksheet (or activity) to indicate the level of effort; the score on the post test as a grade; the improvement shown between a pre-test and post-test as a basis for a grade.

7. Many teachers have stated that the success of an activity may depend on how well students follow directions. Teachers could use this unit to help students develop this important skill.

8. Teachers have found that for many activities the summarizing phase of the instruction is best done at the start of a new day. In this way the summarization can lead into the launch for the next activity and provide a chance for the class to practice new skills, techniques, strategies, and generalizations.

9. Extra challenges are provided in the teacher guide. These can be used for the early finishers, the more able students, or for a review later in the year.

10. The transparencies that are suggested make launching and summarizing quite easy to manage. One could, however, do a good job of these activities with only a few crucial transparencies (for example, a sheet of dot paper).

WHAT THE CAMERA SEES

In this first activity students are introduced to a scheme for recording information about a building built from cubes. The scheme developed is similar to architects' drawings of buildings. It consists of drawing a BASE, a FRONT VIEW and a RIGHT VIEW of the building. These comprise a *set of plans* for the building. In using this scheme, students begin to look at solid objects and pictures of these objects in more discriminating ways. They develop the spatial skill required to ignore their perception of depth and to focus on the outline of the building. They learn visually to distinguish between a left-right reverse of orientation in both two and three dimensions, as shown below.

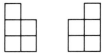

This helps students visualize how a person viewing the opposite side of the building sees it.

In Activity 1, students are provided with both the sets of plans and the buildings. They are asked visually to discriminate among the buildings by looking at each building in three specified ways—BASE, FRONT, and RIGHT—and matching what they see to the sets of plans drawn. Activity 2 gives students the task of drawing sets of plans for given buildings. In Activity 3 the task is reversed: the plans are provided and the students must create a building to match the plans.

All three of these activities provide opportunities for students to practice the basic ideas of seeing and recording used in this scheme. Some students will not be comfortable and confident in using the scheme until all three activities are completed.

Goals for students

1. Look at a building and recognize the FRONT, BACK, RIGHT, and LEFT VIEWS as a camera sees them (without depth perception).
2. Understand what constitutes a set of plans for a building: the BASE is the foundation or outline of the bottom layer; the BACK is the mirror image of the FRONT, and the LEFT is the mirror image of the RIGHT.
3. Develop skill in looking at buildings and matching them to a set of plans.

Activity 1

Materials

Cubes (15 per student in small plastic bags).
Building mat (Worksheet 1-1).
*The Archeologist's Explorations (Materials 1-1).
*The Archeologist's Explorations (continued) (Materials 1-2).
*Mat Plan of First Building (Materials 1-3).
*Mat Plan of Second Building (Materials 1-4).
*Mirror Images of Views (Materials 1-5).
*Launch for Matching Plans (Materials 1-6).
*Matching Summary (Materials 1-7).
*Mats for Buildings (Materials 1-8 to 1-12).
Picture of metropolitan skyline (optional).
Picture of reflections in water (optional).
Mirrors (optional).

Worksheets

1-1, Building Mat.
1-2, Views of First Building.
1-3, Developing Plans for Buildings.
1-4, Matching I—Buildings A, B, C, D, E.
1-5, Matching II—Buildings AA, BB, CC, DD, EE.
*1-6, Mirror Images.
*1-7, Through the Looking Glass.

Transparencies

Starred items should be made into transparencies.

WHAT THE CAMERA SEES

TEACHER ACTION	TEACHER TALK	EXPECTED RESPONSE
Tell the story of an archeologist who discovers a ruin and unlocks the key to reconstructing the building. The text of the story is found on Materials 1-1, The Archeologist's Explorations.		
Display a transparency of the clues the archeologist used, Materials 1-1, 1-2; first show the picture of the foundation and then show the pottery decoration pictures.		
Tell.	The bottom layer of the building left the traces of the foundation.	
	It turned out that these designs were a kind of picture of the building.	
	We are going to learn in the next few activities how to reconstruct buildings from picture-clues like these. Our buildings will be constructed from small cubes instead of stones.	
	Later we'll learn how to make other kinds of pictures of buildings that will allow us to leave a new set of clues about a building for future generations.	

Activity 1 *Launch*

TEACHER ACTION	TEACHER TALK	EXPECTED RESPONSE
Pass out Worksheet 1-1, 1-2, and 15 cubes to each student.		
Explain.	The paper labeled FRONT, BACK, LEFT, and RIGHT is called a Building Mat. Always build on this mat so that you can easily turn it to see the building from all sides. Always position the mat so that the word FRONT is toward you.	BACK / RIGHT / LEFT / FRONT
Display a transparency of the Mat Plan of First Building (Materials 1-3). (1 / 2 / 2 1)	This kind of record of a building is called a *mat plan*.	
	The numbers tell you how high each stack of cubes should be.	
	Take 6 cubes and build the building on your building mat.	
Explain.	Turn the building by turning the building mat, look at it from the front, the right, the back, and the left.	
Display a transparency of Worksheet 1-2.	On Worksheet 1-2 are four pictures of this building.	
	To see what the camera saw when it recorded the pictures, you may need to get down so that your eye is level with the building.	
Ask.	Where was the camera when each of the pictures on Worksheet 1-2 was taken?	LEFT FRONT BACK RIGHT
	Label each picture FRONT, BACK, RIGHT, or LEFT.	
	Notice that the camera does *not* show depth if the picture is taken straight on.	

TEACHER ACTION	TEACHER TALK	EXPECTED RESPONSE
Record students' results on the transparency.	Let's check answers. Where was View 1 taken from?	
	Where was View 2 taken from?	If students have trouble seeing without depth, display a picture of a building on the overhead. Outline the building and then remove the picture to show the shape of the skyline. Pictures of metropolitan skylines cut out of magazines can also help students see that a camera picture taken straight on does not show protrusions toward the camera.
	Where was View 3 taken from?	
	Where was View 4 taken from?	
Students need Worksheet 1-3, Developing Plans for Buildings. Display Mat Plan of Second Building (Materials 1-4) on the overhead.	Now build this building on your building mat.	
	On Worksheet 1-3, Developing Plans for Buildings, draw the foundation of this building in the area labeled **BASE**. Remember that this will be a record of exactly what blocks touch the ground.	
1 3 2 1	Then draw the four views of the building as the camera would see them. Use the areas marked **BACK, FRONT, LEFT, RIGHT**.	
Ask.	Look at Worksheet 1-3. Compare the FRONT and BACK views on each page. Do you see any relationship between them?	They are opposites.
	If I give you the FRONT can you draw the BACK? How?	Some students may immediately see that the two are mirror images or reflections of each other.
	What do you have to do to make them match?	Turn one over.
		If students do not see, ask if they could fit the FRONT on the BACK view if they were allowed to cut the FRONT view out and move it.

Activity 1 *Launch*

TEACHER ACTION	TEACHER TALK	EXPECTED RESPONSE
Ask. Be sure the students see the relationship before posing the next challenge.	What about the RIGHT and LEFT views? Are they paired in any way?	Students should see that these are also mirror images of each other. If the LEFT and RIGHT have been drawn sitting on the same line of the grid, the paper can be folded so that the LEFT falls exactly on the RIGHT side.
Display the building shown below on the overhead or hold up a large picture in front of you (Materials 1-5).	Here is the FRONT view of another building. You are in front of the building and this is what you see. I am in back of the same building. On Worksheet 1-3 in the right-hand grid column, draw what I see.	If students are having trouble, suggest that they build the building and turn it.
Display this building (Materials 1-5).	Here is the RIGHT view of a building and I am on the LEFT side. You see this RIGHT view. Draw what I see.	
Display this building (Materials 1-5).	Here is the FRONT view of a more complicated building. Draw the BACK of the building.	BACK
FRONT		
Flip the transparency over on the overhead to show the correct drawings.	We will call the right and left and front and back *mirror images* or *reflections* of each other.	

11

TEACHER ACTION	TEACHER TALK	EXPECTED RESPONSE

TEACHER ACTION

Display this building on the overhead (Materials 1-5).

RIGHT

Turn the transparency over to show correct answers.

You may want to show pictures from magazines of reflections in water.

Explain.

Display a transparency of Launch for Matching Plans (Materials 1-6) with the three sets of plans covered.

Mat Plan

1	1
2	
3	

TEACHER TALK

Now draw the LEFT view.

We can check these by flipping the transparency over to see the mirror image or the reflection.

Since we always know what the BACK and LEFT views look like if we are given the FRONT and the RIGHT views, we do not need to draw all four views. The FRONT and RIGHT views give the same information as the BACK and LEFT.

We are going to call the three drawings—BASE, FRONT, RIGHT—*a set of plans* for a building. Remember, a set of plans shows *two views* and the *foundation layer*.

This is a *mat plan* for a building. Remember that the numbers tell how high the stacks of cubes are.

Build the building on your mat.

EXPECTED RESPONSE

LEFT

Activity 1 *Launch*

TEACHER ACTION	TEACHER TALK	EXPECTED RESPONSE
Cover the mat plan and expose the three sets of plans.	How can you find out which set of plans matches the building you have built?	
Set 1 BASE FRONT RIGHT		
Set 2 BASE FRONT RIGHT		
Set 3 BASE FRONT RIGHT		
Call on one or two students to suggest strategies.	What would you check first? How does that help?	Various answers. Check the BASE first. This shows that the building plan is set 1 or set 2.
	What would you check next?	Check the FRONT plan. Both sets 1 and 2 have the same FRONT.
	What would you check next?	Check the RIGHT.
	Which is the correct set of plans? Why?	Set 2 matches the building because it matches the BASE, FRONT, and RIGHT.
	How would you verify your answer?	Check all three parts of the set of plans with the building.

TEACHER ACTION

Arrange the class in groups. Students need mats for Buildings A, B, C, D, E (Materials 1-8, 1-9, 1-10), and Worksheet 1-4, Matching I—Buildings A, B, C, D, E. It takes about 50 cubes to build the entire set of buildings at once.

Check to see that all groups have the correct set of buildings.

If time allows, use second matching here. If not, second match can be used at the beginning of day two.

Students need a second set of mats (Materials 1-10, 1-11, 1-12) and Worksheet 1-5, Matching II—Buildings AA, BB, CC, DD, EE.

TEACHER TALK

The first step on your way to becoming an architectural detective is to be able to match plans with buildings.

Each group of students has been given a set of five mats for buildings labeled A, B, C, D, and E.

Place cubes on the mats in the spaces indicated. Make the stack as high as the number in the square.

On your sheet of plans, a set that represents one building is drawn across the page—**BASE, FRONT, RIGHT.**

You are to find the *one* building that fits all *three* of these drawings. Remember to look at the building as if you are a camera.

EXPECTED RESPONSE

Matching I	Matching II
1 C	1 BB
2 D	2 EE
3 E	3 DD
4 B	4 AA
5 A	5 CC

Activity 1 *Launch*

TEACHER ACTION	TEACHER TALK	EXPECTED RESPONSE
Worksheet 1-6, Mirror Images, can be done as a whole class activity or can be given for homework.	This worksheet is about mirror images. Read the instructions carefully. Think of some ways to check your answers.	If students need more direction, illustrate a mirror image problem on the overhead.

If students have difficulty with the Mirror Images worksheet, suggest that they turn the sheet so that the mirror line is vertical and the part already drawn in on their left. Now track around the part drawn with the left index finger one segment at a time as the right hand draws the mirror image, drawing each segment the opposite of the given segment. (Reverse for left handers.)

Using an actual mirror set on the line is another excellent way to check and to help students who are having problems. |
| Worksheet 1-7, Through the Looking Glass, is an extra challenge to be used with students who are ready to tackle an extension of the mirror image idea. | | |

Activity 1 *Summarize*

TEACHER ACTION	TEACHER TALK	EXPECTED RESPONSE
Display a transparency of Materials 1-7. Mat Plan | 3	1	2
1	1	1 | FRONT	Here's a building on which to practice. Build this on your building mat.	
Cover the Mat Plan on the overhead. Reveal the nine views.	Find the FRONT, BACK, RIGHT, and LEFT of the building.	
	Which is the FRONT?	View 5
	Which is the BACK?	View 7
	Which is the RIGHT?	View 9
	Which is the LEFT?	View 4
	What strategies did you use to find the correct views?	Various answers.
	What ways did you find to check the mirror image sheets?	Various answers, such as use a mirror, fold on line, and hold to light.
	How do we use mirror images to help decide what to draw in a set of plans?	FRONT and BACK, RIGHT and LEFT are mirror images of each other so we only draw the FRONT and RIGHT.
	The base is the bottom layer, not a view. Sometimes that makes a difference. We used the view from the front and the view from the *right* side.	
Discuss Worksheet 1-6, Mirror Images, and again emphasize why we do not need to draw both the front *and* back, right *and* left.		

The Archeologist's Explorations

An archeologist exploring a small isolated island has found the ruins of an ancient building. The mystery building had been made from large cubes of stone cut from the island quarry. The stones are scattered around the immediate area of the foundation of the building. The terrain and remoteness of the island suggest that no stones have been removed from the area.

There is a clear outline of the foundation of the building left in the ground.

Outline of the Base of the Archeologist's Mystery Building

Copyright © 1986 Addison-Wesley Publishing Company, Inc.

The Archeologist's Explorations (continued)

An experimental area is excavated between the wings of the foundation. Among the pots unearthed are several ceremonial pots and plates with square, geometric designs. They appear to belong with the building. In the past archeologists have found that the designs on such ceremonial pots are often pictorial records of the times.

On several of the plates the designs are the same. The archeologist believes that the designs on the plates are views of the building that once stood on the foundation. Here are the designs. Can you reconstruct the archeologist's mystery building?

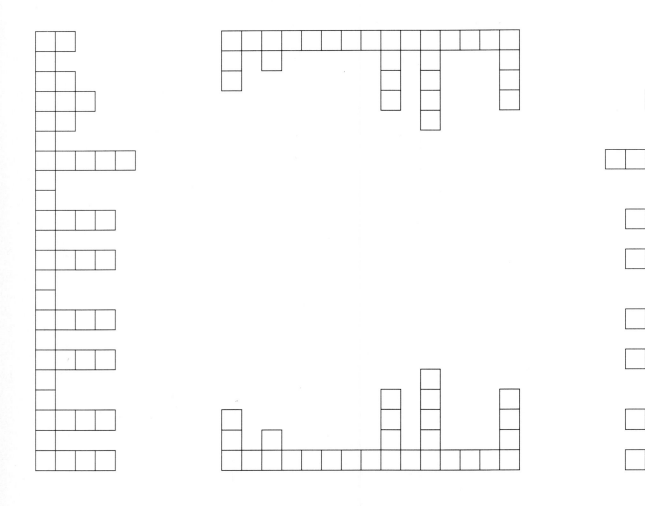

Mat Plan of First Building

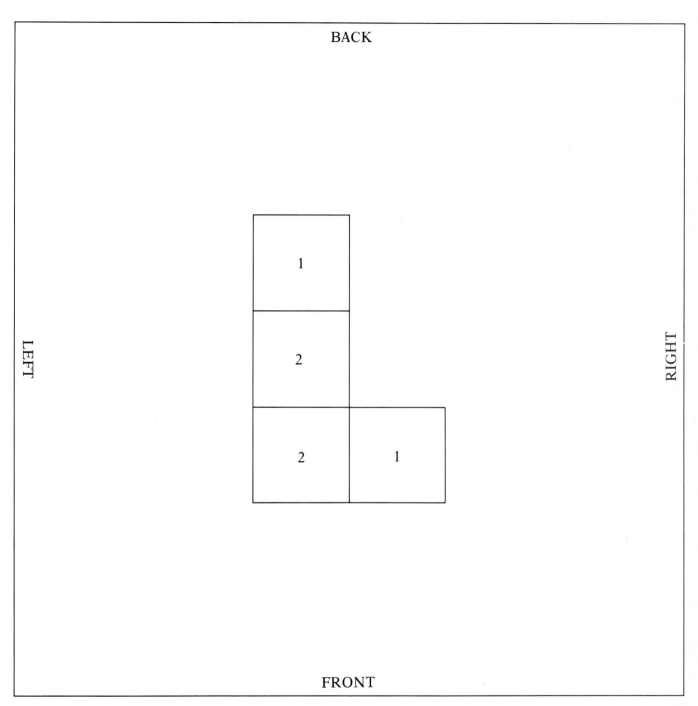

Mat Plan of Second Building

BACK

LEFT

RIGHT

1	
3	
2	1

FRONT

Mirror Images of Views

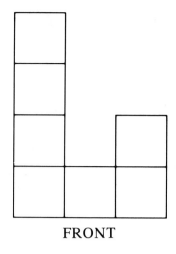

FRONT

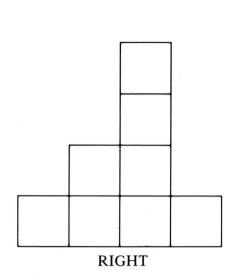

RIGHT

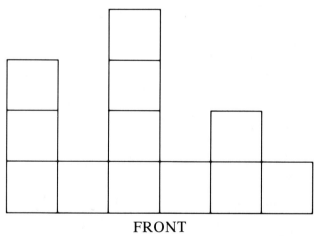

FRONT

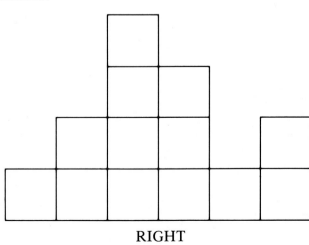

RIGHT

Launch for Matching Plans

Mat Plan

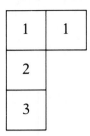

Sets of Plans

Set 1

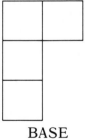

BASE

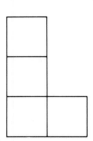

FRONT

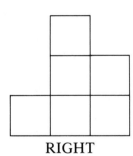

RIGHT

Set 2

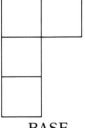

BASE

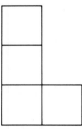

FRONT

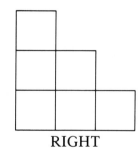

RIGHT

Set 3

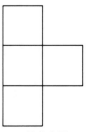

BASE

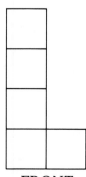

FRONT

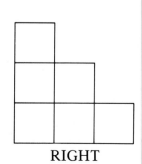

RIGHT

Matching Summary

Mat Plan

	3	
1	1	2
1	1	1

FRONT

Views

1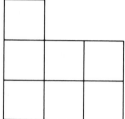

2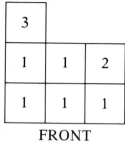

3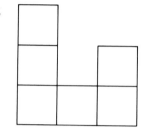

4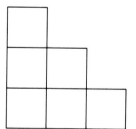

5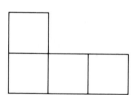

6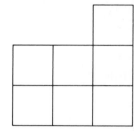

7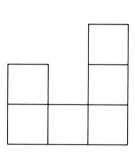

8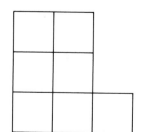

9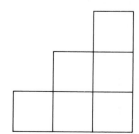

Materials 1-8

Building A

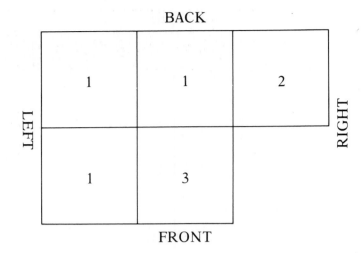

Building B

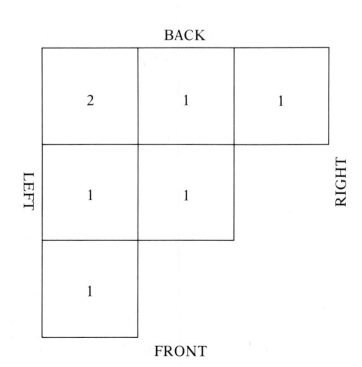

Materials 1-9

Building C

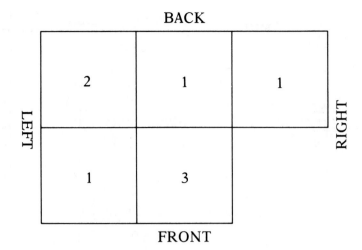

Building D

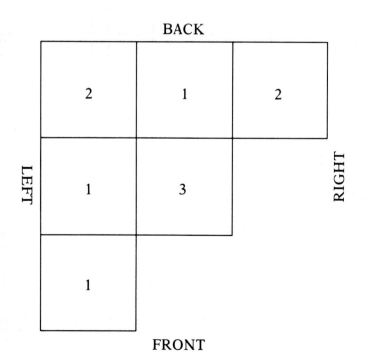

Materials 1-10

Building E

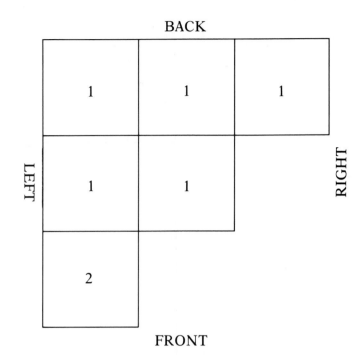

Building AA

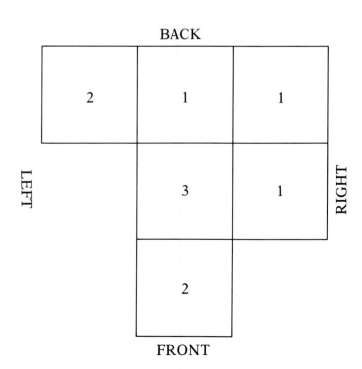

Building BB

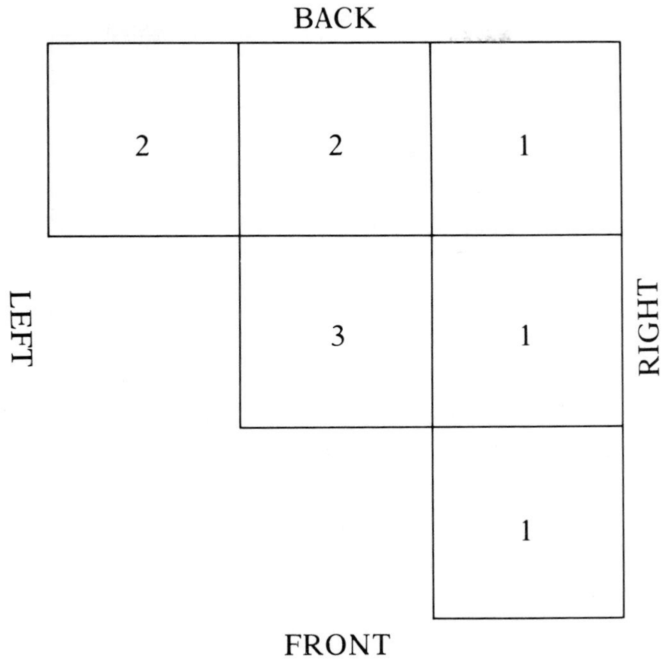

BACK

2	2	1
	3	1
		1

LEFT

RIGHT

FRONT

Building CC

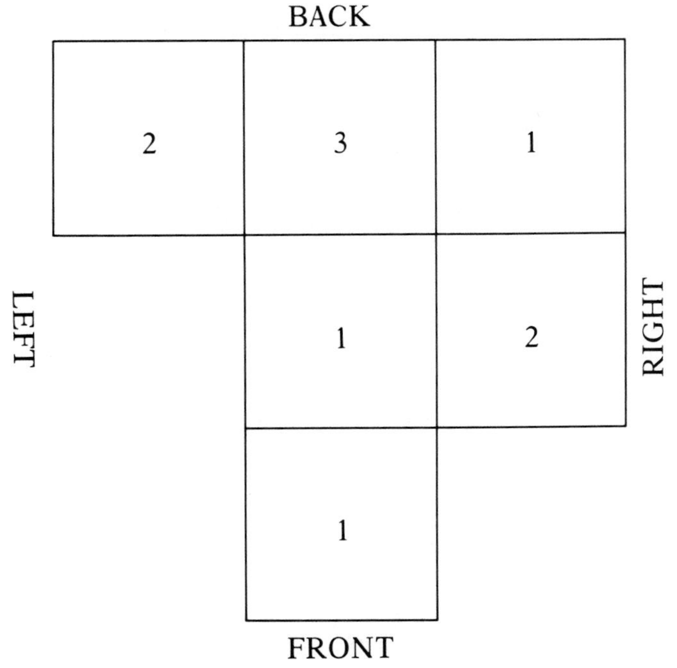

BACK

2	3	1
	1	2
	1	

LEFT

RIGHT

FRONT

Building DD

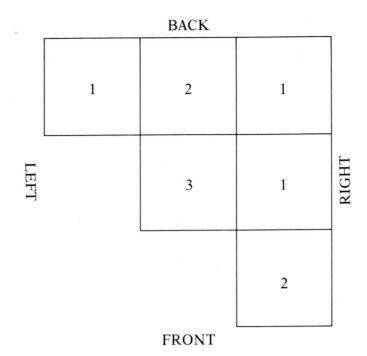

Building EE

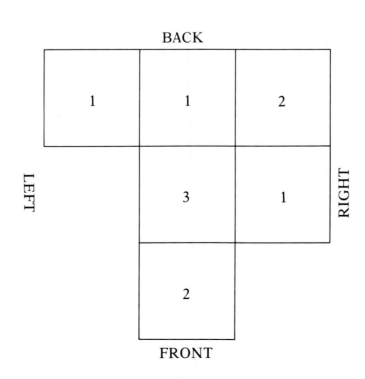

Building Mat

BACK

LEFT

RIGHT

FRONT

Views of First Building

1

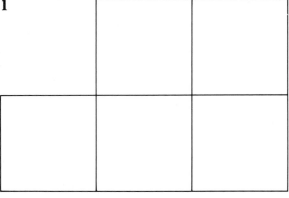

2

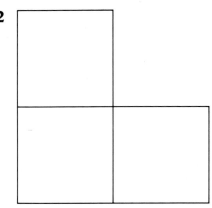

3

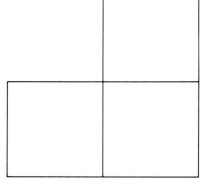

4

Worksheet 1-2

Developing Plans for Buildings

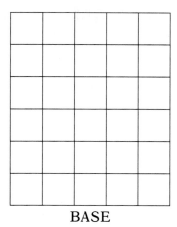

BASE

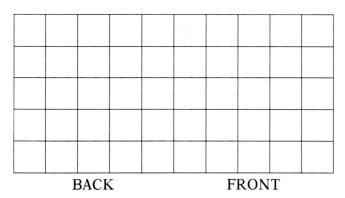

BACK   FRONT

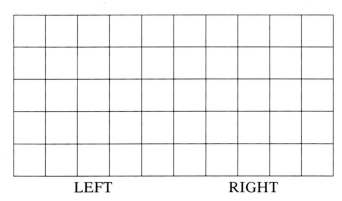

LEFT   RIGHT

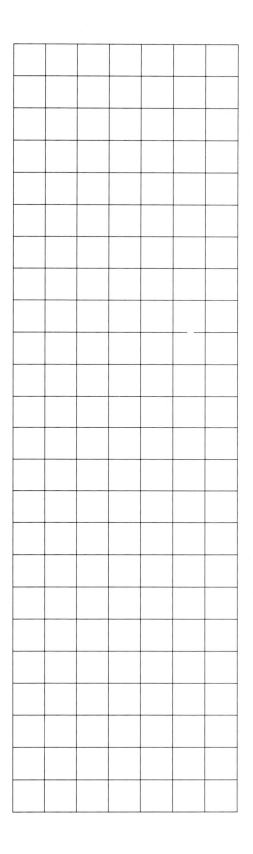

Matching I—
Buildings A, B, C, D, E

On the mats provided, construct buildings A, B, C, D, E. Match each set of plans—BASE, FRONT, RIGHT—with the correct building.

Set 1

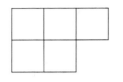

BASE
(Front at Bottom)

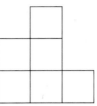

FRONT

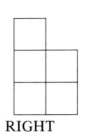

RIGHT

Matches building

_____

Set 2

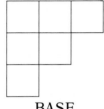

BASE

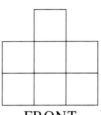

FRONT

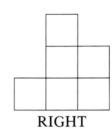

RIGHT

Matches building

_____

Set 3

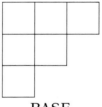

BASE

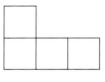

FRONT

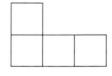

RIGHT

Matches building

_____

Set 4

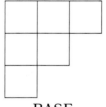

BASE

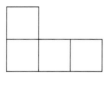

FRONT

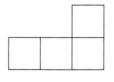

RIGHT

Matches building

_____

Set 5

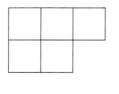

BASE

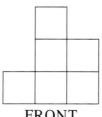

FRONT

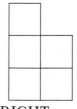

RIGHT

Matches building

_____

Worksheet 1-4

NAME _____

Matching II—
Buildings AA, BB, CC, DD, EE

On the mats provided, construct buildings AA, BB, CC, DD, EE.
Match each set of plans—BASE, FRONT, RIGHT—with the correct
building.

Set 1

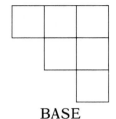
BASE
(Front at Bottom)

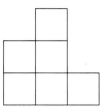
FRONT

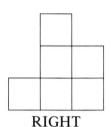
RIGHT

Matches building

_____

Set 2

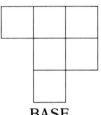
BASE

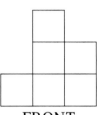
FRONT

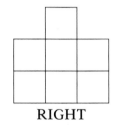
RIGHT

Matches building

_____

Set 3

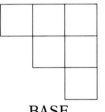
BASE

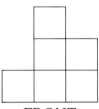
FRONT

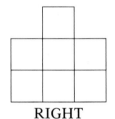
RIGHT

Matches building

_____

Set 4

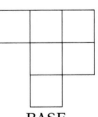
BASE

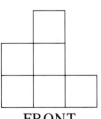
FRONT

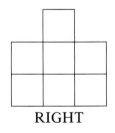
RIGHT

Matches building

_____

Set 5

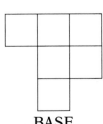
BASE

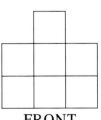
FRONT

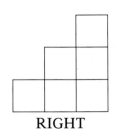
RIGHT

Matches building

_____

MATHEMATICS DEPARTMENT
ALVERNO COLLEGE
MILWAUKEE, WI 53234-3922

Mirror Images

In each of these pictures is a mirror line. Everything on one side of the mirror will appear to be on the other side, too. Put in everything exactly as it would appear in the mirror.

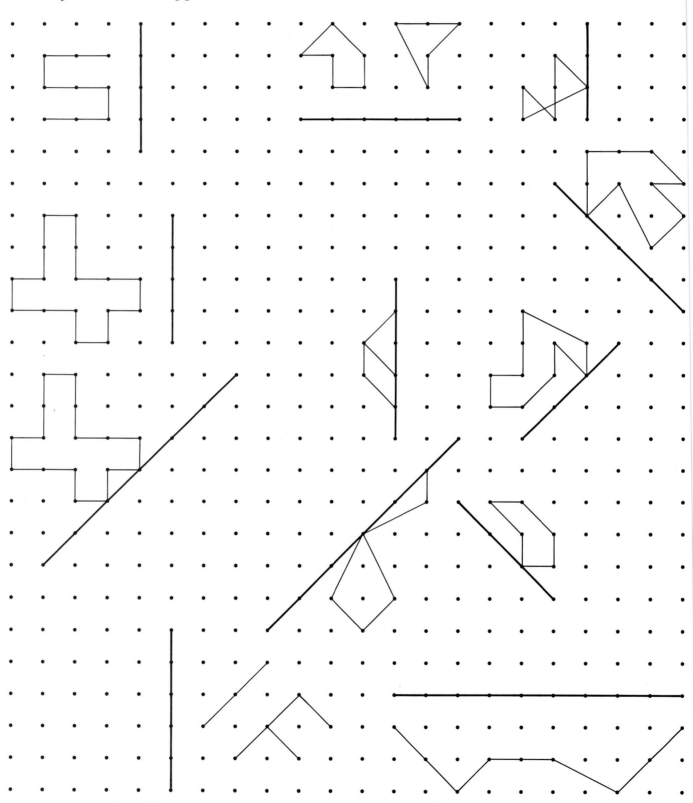

Worksheet 1-6

Through the Looking Glass

In these pictures you are shown part of what is on each side of the mirror. Complete the picture so that each side is the mirror image of the other.

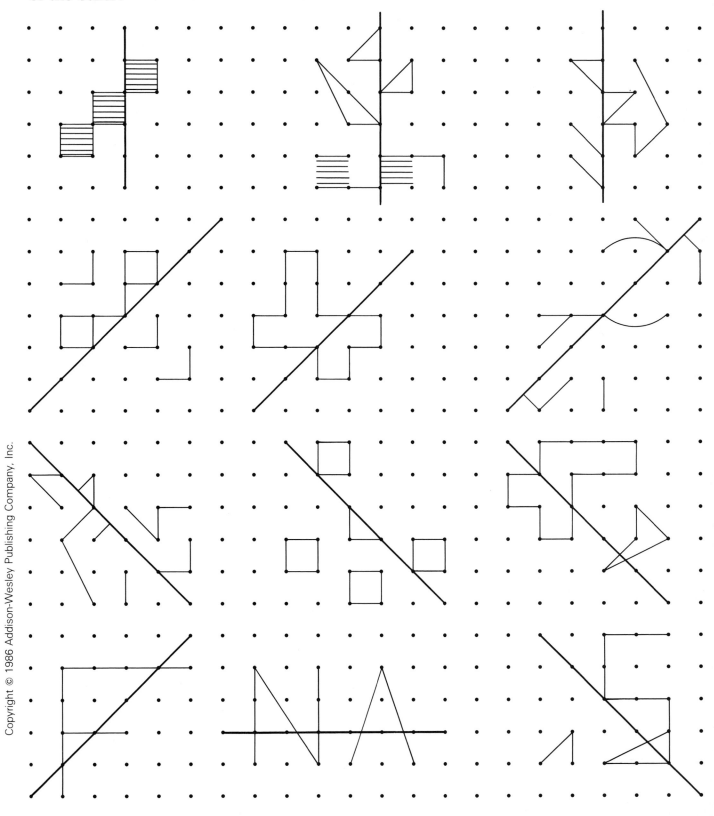

Activity 2

DRAWING PLANS OF BUILDINGS

OVERVIEW

Students' ability to comprehend what they read is enhanced by writing stories of their own. In the same way, drawing sets of plans for buildings increases a student's ability to read information from a three-dimensional object and translate what they see into a flat picture. Drawing sets of plans requires a deeper understanding of the architectural scheme than is revealed in simply matching an object to a set of correctly drawn plans. A student must realize the importance of orienting the three drawings that comprise a set of plans so that they can be properly read in relation to each other. The BASE must be drawn as one would see it looking from the FRONT. The FRONT and RIGHT views must be drawn with the same orientation that is seen when looking at the building, not turned in any way. This gives a consistency to the three parts of a plan, which allows students to read the information back to recreate the building.

The spatial skills involved in this activity are interesting. In looking at a building and in reading a set of plans the student must deal with perpendicular planes in space. The BASE represents information about the building in a horizontal plane, while the FRONT and RIGHT are views of the building in vertical planes perpendicular to the base.

Giving the students incomplete plans for buildings provides a bridge between drawing plans and reading plans. Here the student must read the partial plans, create a building that fits, draw the remaining part of the plans, and then check to see that the set of plans and the building match.

Goals for students

1. Learn to draw sets of plans for an existing building.
2. Understand that the BASE, FRONT, and RIGHT views must be oriented in a consistent way so that the set of plans can be read correctly to recreate the building.
3. Understand through incomplete plans the process of reading from sets of plans to create a building.
4. Create a building by reading from sets of incomplete plans.

Materials

Cubes.
*Summary of Drawing Plans (Materials 2-2).
Mats for Buildings F, G, H, I (Materials 2-3, 2-4).
Building Mat (Worksheet 1-1).

Worksheets

*2-1, Drawing Plans.
2-2, Incomplete Plans.

Transparencies

Starred items should be made into transparencies.

DRAWING PLANS OF BUILDINGS

TEACHER ACTION	TEACHER TALK	EXPECTED RESPONSE
Set the scene.	In Activity 1 we developed a set of plans to describe a three-dimensional building by drawing a BASE plan and a FRONT and RIGHT view. In this activity we will practice drawing a set of plans for a given building.	
Pass out cubes. Each student will need at least 11 cubes.	Place your building mat on your desk.	
Give directions.	Build this building on your mat.	
Display a transparency of Drawing Plans (Materials 2-1).		

```
BACK
┌───┐
│ 1 │
├───┤
│ 2 │
├───┤
│ 3 │
├───┬───┬───┐
│ 2 │ 2 │ 1 │
└───┴───┴───┘
LEFT        FRONT   RIGHT
```

TEACHER ACTION	TEACHER TALK	EXPECTED RESPONSE
Expose only the first set of plans.	Look carefully at the building you have constructed.	
	Could this be a correct set of plans for the building?	Various answers. Give students time to think. If they immediately say "No," ask why. Set 1 is not correct because the BASE is not oriented correctly.
	Remember: The base must be drawn *from the* front.	
	Could these be the plans of any building?	You cannot place a FRONT that is only three units wide onto a BASE that is four units wide.

Activity 2 *Launch*

TEACHER ACTION	TEACHER TALK	EXPECTED RESPONSE
Reveal set 2. Ask.	What do you think about this set of plans? Does it match the building?	No, the RIGHT is incorrectly drawn. It's floating.
	What do you think the student who drew this plan had in mind when he drew the cube hanging down?	He was trying to show that one cube is in front of another.
Explain.	Remember that the FRONT and RIGHT are *views* of the building and should be always thought of as "standing up." The RIGHT view drawn here would be impossible. The building would fall down.	
Be sure to *remove* the transparency from the overhead.		
Students need Worksheet 2-1, Drawing Plans. Give directions.	Now draw on the back of Worksheet 2-1 a correct set of plans for this building.	BASE FRONT RIGHT
After everyone has done this, reveal the last set of plans on the overhead.	Is this what you drew?	Yes!
	How can we check to see if we have the correct drawings?	Look at the building and check each part.
Review.	The things to watch are 1) the orientation of the base—the base is always drawn from the front; 2) the base is the bottom layer or foundation; 3) the FRONT and RIGHT view *do not* show depth perception; 4) the height of the stacks in the rows in both the FRONT and RIGHT views—they should match.	

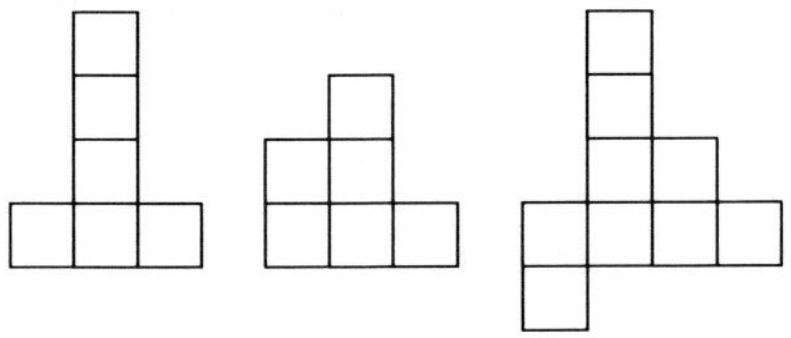

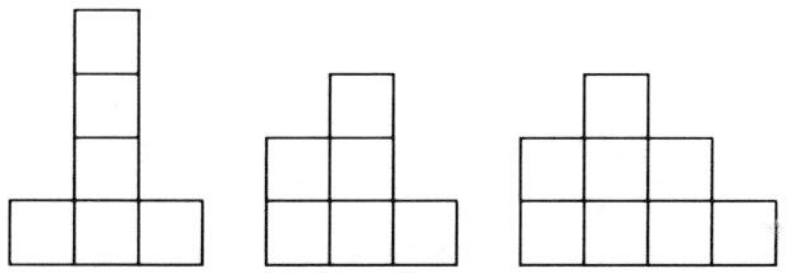

Activity 2 *Explore*

TEACHER ACTION

Have students work in groups on Worksheet 2-1. Students need base mats for building F, G, H, and I.

Hold up model of tower.

A large number of students will orient the base of G (the sling shot) incorrectly. Remind them that when the BASE is turned it is not a correct set of plans.

A large number of students will draw 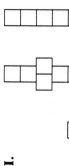 for the base of building I. Remind them that the BASE is what touches the paper.

TEACHER TALK

In your groups first construct the four buildings to be drawn.

Building I is a tower that looks like this.

Draw a set of plans for each building.

EXPECTED RESPONSE

Students should draw these plans.

F.

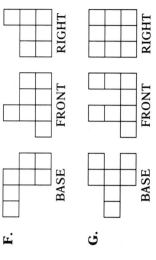

BASE   FRONT   RIGHT

G.

BASE   FRONT   RIGHT

H.

BASE   FRONT   RIGHT

I.

BASE   FRONT   RIGHT

40

Activity 2 *Summarize*

TEACHER ACTION	TEACHER TALK	EXPECTED RESPONSE
Worksheet 2-2, Incomplete Plans, provides a link between this activity, *Drawing Plans*, and the next activity, which is *Building From Plans*.		
Begin by summarizing the drawing. Elicit several responses.	Give me one thing that you had to be careful about when drawing plans.	Orientation of BASE; orientation of views; depth perception; BASE is the foundation, not a view. On building I, the layer of two cubes must *not* be like this.
Students need Worksheet 2-2, Incomplete Plans.	Let's do number 1 on your Incomplete Plans worksheet together.	
	On your building mat, make a base of cubes like the base given in number 1.	
	Now that the base is established, no other cubes can touch your building mat. Add other cubes on top of the base to make the view from the right match the view given.	
	Make a record of your building by writing the height numbers in the squares of the base. Remember, this is called a mat plan.	

Activity 2 *Summarize*

TEACHER ACTION	TEACHER TALK	EXPECTED RESPONSE

Collect several solutions for number 1 and display on the overhead.

If all the students give this solution

ask if they can add another cube and still fit the **BASE** and **RIGHT**; how many additional cubes can be used and still fit the **BASE** and **RIGHT**?

After doing one problem together you can either continue the worksheet as a whole class activity, or have the students work individually or in groups and then summarize their results.

Many students find the two problems with a missing base more difficult. If a student is stuck, focus attention on such questions as "How wide does the base have to be from the front?" "Where should you see a stack of three high as you look at the **FRONT** or at the **RIGHT**?" "What location on the base would satisfy both requirements?" (first row, three cubes back)

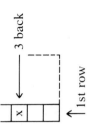

Some students will discover that a rectangle as wide as the **FRONT** and as long as the **RIGHT** will always work. This would give

for number 3   and   for number 4.

Drawing Plans

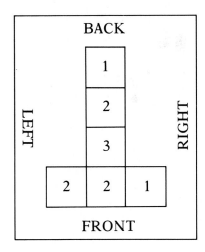

Set 1

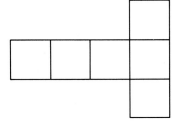

BASE

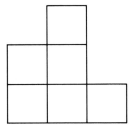

FRONT

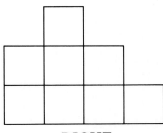

RIGHT

Set 2

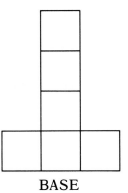

BASE

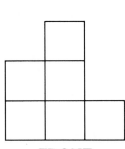

FRONT

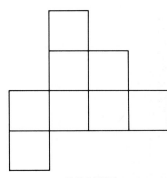

RIGHT

Set 3

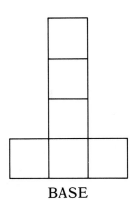

BASE

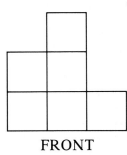

FRONT

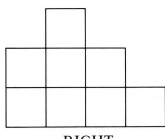

RIGHT

Summary Drawing Plans

Building F

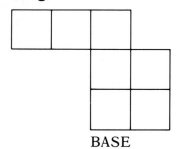

BASE

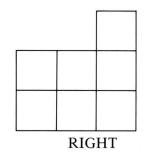

FRONT

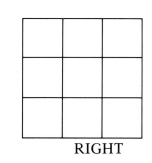

RIGHT

Building G

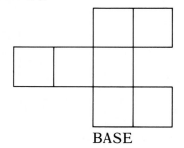

BASE

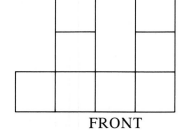

FRONT

RIGHT

Building H

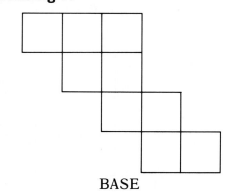

BASE

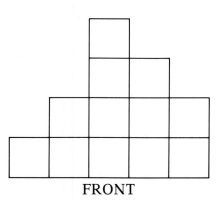

FRONT

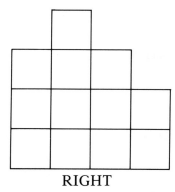

RIGHT

Building I

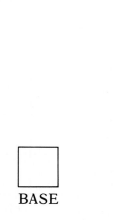

BASE

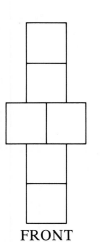

FRONT

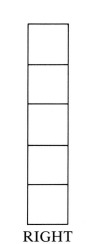

RIGHT

Building F

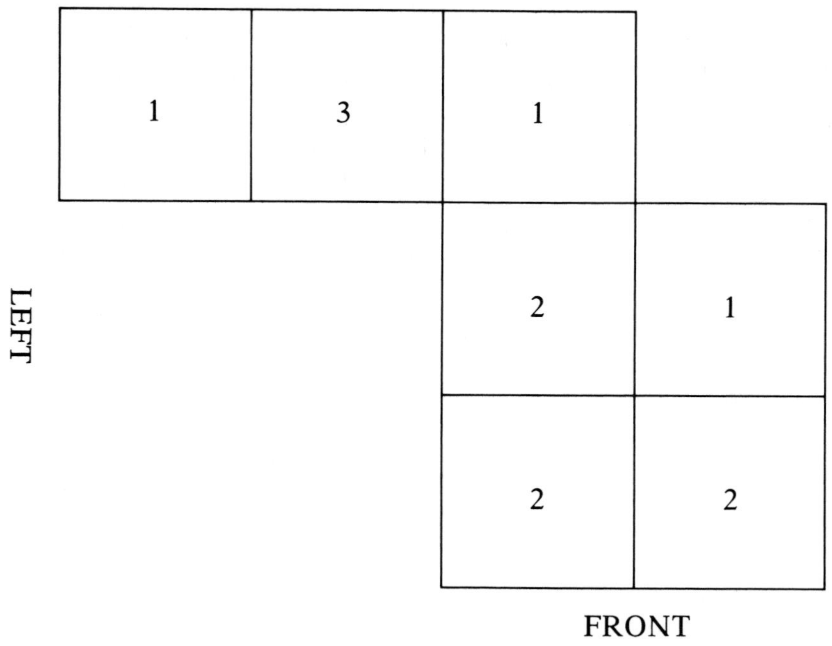 1	3	1

2	1
2	2

FRONT

LEFT

Building G

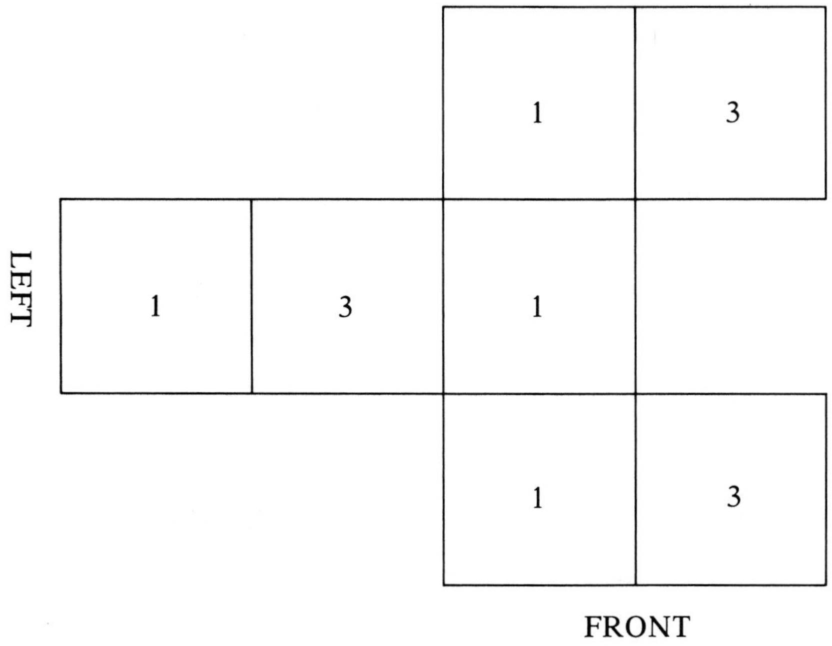 1	3

1	3	1

1	3

LEFT

FRONT

Building H

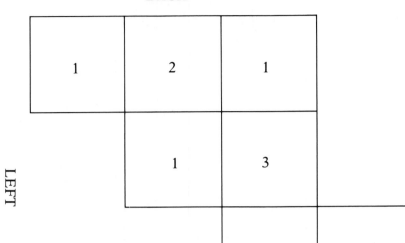

BACK

LEFT

RIGHT

FRONT

1	2	1

Building I (tower)

LEFT

FRONT

NAME

Drawing Plans

F.

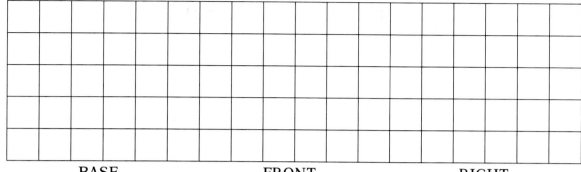

BASE   FRONT   RIGHT

G.

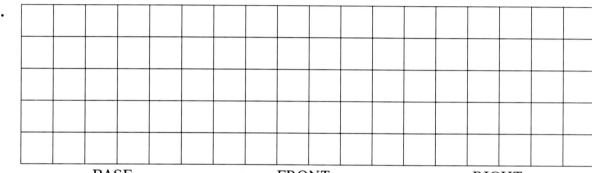

BASE   FRONT   RIGHT

H.

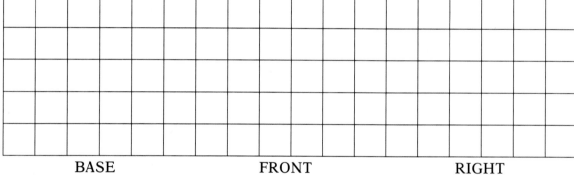

BASE   FRONT   RIGHT

I.

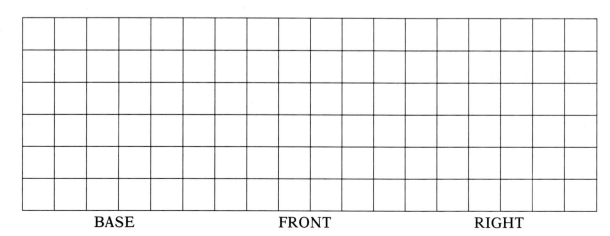

BASE   FRONT   RIGHT

Incomplete Plans

1. Create a building that has this BASE and RIGHT. Draw its FRONT. Record your building on a mat plan.

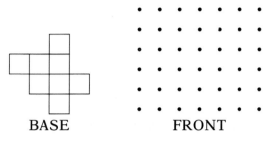

BASE   FRONT   RIGHT

2. Create a building that has this BASE and FRONT. Draw its RIGHT. Record your building on a mat plan.

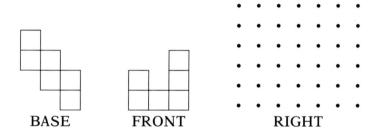

BASE   FRONT   RIGHT

3. Create a building that has this FRONT and RIGHT. Draw its BASE. Record your building on a mat plan.

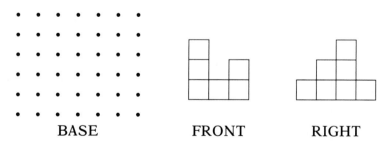

BASE   FRONT   RIGHT

4. Create a building that has this FRONT and RIGHT. Draw its BASE. Record your building on a mat plan.

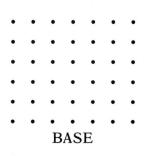
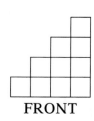
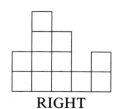

BASE   FRONT   RIGHT

BUILDING FROM PLANS

Copyright © 1986 Addison-Wesley Publishing Company, Inc.

OVERVIEW

This activity poses the opposite challenge to that of Activity 2. Here the plans are provided and the students must create a building that fits the plans. For some students, efficient strategies for constructing buildings emerge slowly. One frequent beginning strategy is to attempt the construction by building first the BASE and then the entire FRONT. These students are often surprised when they turn the building to look at the RIGHT and see that it does *not* match. This strategy is soon replaced by a much more efficient strategy of using the FRONT and RIGHT views simultaneously when placing the cubes.

   As the students build and make records of their buildings, many will discover that a set of plans may not produce a *unique* building. The fact that several buildings may have the same set of plans is explored in the next activity.

Goals for students

I. Develop an efficient strategy for reading a set of plans and for constructing a building that fits it.

Materials

Cubes.
Building Mat (Worksheet 1-1).
*Drawing Plans (Materials 2-1).

Worksheets

*3-1, Building from Plans.
1-4, Matching I—Buildings A, B, C, D, E.

Transparencies

Starred items should be made into transparencies.

BUILDING FROM PLANS

TEACHER ACTION	TEACHER TALK	EXPECTED RESPONSE
Pass out cubes and Worksheet 3-1, Building From Plans.	We have drawn plans of existing buildings. Now we'll go the other way.	
Display a transparency of Materials 2-1, Drawing Plans.	Construct a building that fits these plans.	
Set 3 BASE FRONT RIGHT		
Explain.	To record our building, we'll make a mat plan from the drawing of the base.	
	What goes here?	
	There would be a 2 or 1 in the last space. Sometimes there is more than one way to make a building.	
1 2 3 2 1	As you build each of the buildings J through P make a mat plan on the base given.	
Homework suggestion: Worksheet 3-1 could be cut after buildings N and O; buildings P, Q, R, and S could be used as an extra challenge or omitted.	Mat plans won't work for Q, R, and S.	

Activity 3 *Explore*

TEACHER ACTION	TEACHER TALK	EXPECTED RESPONSE

TEACHER ACTION

Walk around and check.

Check Q, R, and S visually or have a set built and let students check their own.

Some students will begin with naive strategies, such as building the BASE and the entire FRONT before checking the RIGHT. Encourage these students to use the FRONT and RIGHT *together* to decide where stacks of cubes must be placed.

Occasionally students will be able to read plans so well that they can make a mat plan *without* building. These students should be encouraged to build some of the buildings to practice visually checking the solid object against the set of plans.

EXPECTED RESPONSE

Students build.

A 1 or 2 may be placed in each of the empty cells, provided that each row and column marked with an asterisk has a 2 somewhere.

L.

M.

N.

O.

P.

Q.

R.

S.

TEACHER ACTION	TEACHER TALK	EXPECTED RESPONSE

For early finishers, Worksheet 1-4, Matching I—Buildings A, B, C, D, E, can be used again. Have students try to make mat plans without actually constructing the buildings.

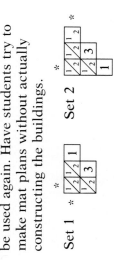

Set 1

Set 2

Set 3

Set 4

Set 5

Building from Plans

Use the plans to construct Buildings J–S. Use the BASE of each set
of plans to make a mat plan record of your building.

J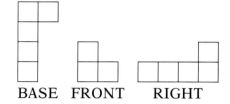
BASE   FRONT   RIGHT

K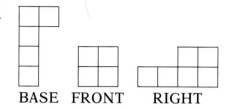
BASE FRONT   RIGHT

L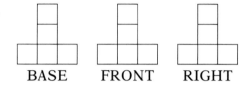
BASE   FRONT   RIGHT

M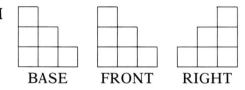
BASE   FRONT   RIGHT

N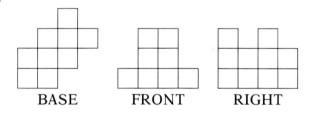
BASE   FRONT   RIGHT

O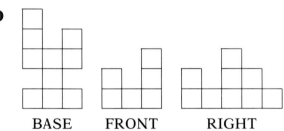
BASE   FRONT   RIGHT

P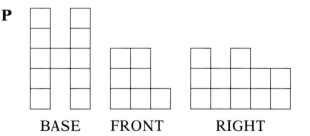
BASE   FRONT   RIGHT

Q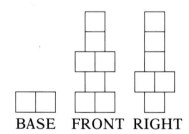
BASE FRONT RIGHT

R (non-standard base)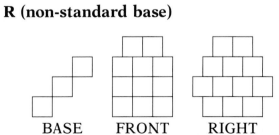
BASE   FRONT   RIGHT

S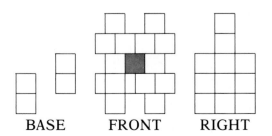
BASE   FRONT   RIGHT

UNIQUENESS PLANS

OVERVIEW

The scheme we have used for giving information about a building does not describe a unique building. In this activity we explore this lack of uniqueness by looking at all the buildings that fit a particular set of plans. Among the buildings, we are most interested in the *minimal buildings*, those built with the fewest possible cubes, and *maximal buildings*, those built with the most cubes. The culmination of the activity is to elicit from the students that while there may be several different minimal buildings for a set of plans, the maximal building is unique. Mystery Buildings I and II provide a final challenge and use the notion that all groups will produce the same building because a maximal building is required. This is an excellent final practice in using the scheme, since the students must be constantly mindful of keeping the building true to the set of plans while adding, moving, and removing cubes.

A discussion of surface area and volume could follow this activity.

Goals for students

1. Recognize that a set of plans may not produce a unique building.
2. Determine which cubes are *fixed* for all versions of a set of plans.
3. Understand that a set of plans may have several *minimal* buildings, but only one *maximal* building.

Materials

Cubes.
Building Mat (Worksheet 1-1).
*Uniqueness Plans (Materials 4-1).

Worksheets

*4-1, Minimal and Maximal.
4-2, Mystery Building I.
4-3, Mystery Building II (optional).

Transparencies

Starred items should be made into transparencies.

TEACHER ACTION	TEACHER TALK	EXPECTED RESPONSE
Pass out cubes. Display a transparency of Materials 4-1, Uniqueness Plans, on the overhead.	Build a building that fits these plans.	Students will produce one of several possible buildings.
BASE FRONT RIGHT		
Ask.	Is there a different way you could have built it?	Yes.
	In what ways do the buildings differ?	Some have more cubes than others; some have cubes in different places.
Explain.	Once we have a building that fits the plans we can sometimes add cubes, remove cubes, or possibly move cubes and still have a building that fits.	
Give directions. Draw a mat for one of the buildings to illustrate how to keep a record.	Let's find them all. On a piece of paper draw the mats for each building that you find.	
Record students' results.	On the overhead let's record every building that you found.	
Ask.	Are there any squares on the mat that are always the same?	The middle one.
	That cube is *fixed*. It cannot be changed and still have a building to match the set of plans.	

Activity 4 *Launch*

TEACHER ACTION	TEACHER TALK	EXPECTED RESPONSE
When you are satisfied with the student responses, ask.	What is the greatest number of cubes needed?	Nine.
	We call this a *maximal building*.	
	What is the smallest number of blocks needed?	Seven.
	This is a *minimal building*.	
	How many minimal buildings are there?	Two.
	How many maximal buildings are there?	One.
	Could there be more than one maximal building?	Various answers. It is not important to resolve this question until after the exploration.

Activity 4 *Explore*

TEACHER ACTION	TEACHER TALK	EXPECTED RESPONSE
	There are three different sets of plans on your worksheet. For each, you are to find a minimal and maximal building.	
If students have only 15 cubes each, they must work in pairs.		
Ask early finishers to make as many different mat plans for building U as possible (10).		
Ask others to do the same for building W (9).		

Activity 4 *Summarize*

TEACHER ACTION	TEACHER TALK	EXPECTED RESPONSE
Put plans of the buildings U, V, W (Materials 4-2) on the overhead.	How many cubes for the maximal building?	**Building U**
Collect and record a maximal solution and a minimal solution for each building.		Minimal 12 Maximal 15
	Any other minimal plans?	Various answers.
	Does anyone have a different maximal plan?	**Building V**
		Minimal 15 Maximal 19
		Building W
		Minimal 19 Maximal 23
	Now what do you think? Is the maximal building unique? Why?	Yes, because if someone has a cube that you don't have, you can add it.

Building U — Minimal 12:
```
1
3
  1 2 1
2 1 1
2 2
```

Building U — Maximal 15:
```
1
3
  2 2 1
2 2 2
2 2
```

Building V — Minimal 15:
```
1
1 1 3 2
1 2 1
    2 1
```

Building V — Maximal 19:
```
1
2 2 3 2
1 2 2
    2 2
```

Building W — Minimal 19:
```
      1 1 3
1 1 1 1
1 4 1
  1 3
  1 1
```

Building W — Maximal 23:
```
      3 1 3
1 1 3 1
1 4 1 3
  1 3
  1 1
```

Activity 4 *Summarize*

TEACHER ACTION

Pass out Worksheet 4-2, Mystery Building I.

Have early finishers take away cubes to get the minimal building. How many cubes are needed for the minimal building? (41)

Worksheet 4-3, Mystery Building II, may be done now or saved for review. As an extra challenge, ask students to find the minimal number of cubes needed. (42)

TEACHER TALK

We're just about ready to work on the archeologist's problem. Let's look at the foundation and the pottery designs again. Any ideas about how to interpret these designs?

Here is a similar building whose remains and some pottery clues were found on nearby islands. Pathways and a mark on the pottery indicated which side was the front of the building.

Work in groups of four and build a maximal building. Record your building.

Write down how many cubes you needed.

EXPECTED RESPONSE

The FRONT and BACK and LEFT and RIGHT views are on the borders.

48. If student answers are too small, stress *maximal* building.

Uniqueness Plans

BASE

FRONT

RIGHT

Minimal and Maximal

1. Find the number of cubes needed to construct a minimal building and the number of cubes needed to construct a maximal building. Make a mat plan for each.

Building U

Minimal Mat Plan _____

Maximal Mat Plan _____

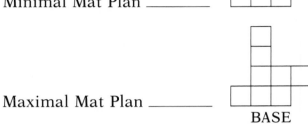

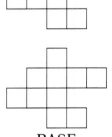

BASE

FRONT   RIGHT

Building V

Minimal Mat Plan _____

Maximal Mat Plan _____

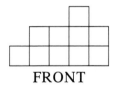

BASE

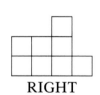

FRONT   RIGHT

Building W

Minimal Mat Plan _____

Maximal Mat Plan _____

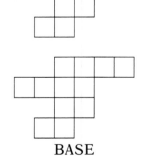

BASE

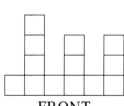

FRONT   RIGHT

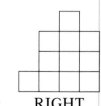

2. Can you find a different mat plan for the maximal building?

Mystery Building I

This is a drawing of the foundation of the Mystery Building.

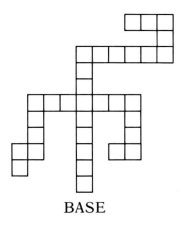

BASE

These are the pottery views of the building.

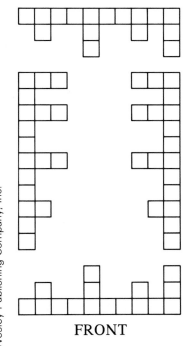

FRONT

Construct a *maximal* version of the Mystery Building and make a mat plan of the results on the drawing of the foundation.

Number of cubes needed _____

Mystery Building II

This is a drawing of the foundation of the Mystery Building.

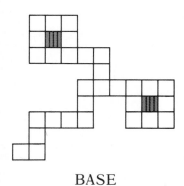

BASE

These are the pottery views of the building.

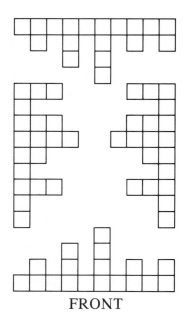

FRONT

Construct a *maximal* version of the Mystery Building and make a mat plan of the results on the drawing of the foundation.

Number of cubes needed _____

Worksheet 4-3

Activity 5

INTRODUCTION TO ISOMETRIC DOT PAPER

OVERVIEW

This activity introduces another way of looking at buildings and recording what is seen. In the first scheme a building was viewed so that only one face was seen at a time. Now the buildings are turned and viewed from a corner, so that three faces of the building show simultaneously. Students often have to deal with pictures of this sort in textbooks, but many cannot read these three-dimensional pictures well enough to determine the needed information about the solid objects. For example, how many cubes are needed to build this solid?

Students make two types of errors. They count the faces of every cube showing and answer 16, or they count only the cubes showing and answer 10. To answer correctly the students must be able to visualize the hidden corner of the solid.

These activities were designed to provide concrete experiences in dealing with these three-dimensional pictures. The students learn to read and to make drawings of buildings on isometric dot paper (paper with dots arranged on diagonals rather than rows). Our experiences in teaching these activities to students led us to develop a language for moves on the dot paper. This language of moves allows the teacher and the students to communicate precisely about the buildings and drawings. The language becomes an especially valuable tool in helping a student with poor spatial skills begin to produce drawings of simple buildings.

Activity 5 introduces isometric dot paper and the language of legal moves. The students are given an opportunity to build simple buildings, copy isometric drawings of the buildings, and answer questions about numbers of cubes needed to build the buildings.

Goals for students

1. Learn allowable moves on isometric dot paper; only slant and vertical lines are allowed, no horizontal lines.
2. Learn to use the language of the moves to describe a path on isometric dot paper.
3. Learn to copy figures on isometric dot paper.

Materials

Cubes.

*Isometric Dot Paper (Materials 5-1).

Building BB (for demonstration) (Worksheet 7-1).

Worksheets

*5-1, Dot Paper Moves.

*5-2, Copy Figures.

*5-3, Figures and Paths.

Transparencies

Starred items should be made into transparencies.

TEACHER ACTION	TEACHER TALK	EXPECTED RESPONSE
Students need a piece of Isometric Dot Paper (Materials 5-1). Before you begin this activity, let the students become familiar with the isometric dot paper by allowing them a few minutes to draw anything they like on the dot paper.		
Hold up building BB and show pictures of building BB drawn on isometric dot paper. Use a transparency of Worksheet 7-1.	We are going to learn a new way to draw pictures of buildings. This picture is an example. We will use paper with dots arranged in a special pattern.	
Display a transparency of isometric dot paper.	Do you see anything special or different about this paper compared to other dot paper you have used?	Various answers. Dots are not arranged in horizontal rows; they are arranged on diagonals.
Give directions.	Place your pencil on a dot on your dot paper. Some of the dots are nearest neighbors to your dot. Draw a line segment to a nearest neighbor.	
Follow student response on the overhead.		
Give directions.	Now, draw line segments to connect your dot to each of its nearest neighbors.	
	The line segments we have drawn are all the same length.	
	This kind of dot paper takes its name from this picture that you have drawn. The paper is called *isometric dot paper*.	
	What do you think this word means?	Various answers.

TEACHER ACTION	TEACHER TALK	EXPECTED RESPONSE
Explain.	The prefix *iso-* means "equal" and *metric* means "measure." So, *isometric* means "equal measure." The nearest neighbors of a dot are an equal distance away from the dot.	
Classify.	These nearest neighbor lines are the only lines that you are allowed to draw from any dot.	
Draw and then label on the overhead.	You can draw *up*, U.	
	You can draw *down*, D.	
	You can draw a slant line *up and to the right*, U_R.	
	You can draw a slant line *up and to the left*, U_L.	
	You can draw a slant line *down and to the right*, D_R.	
	You can draw a slant line *down and to the left*, D_L.	
	Horizontal lines are *not* allowed!	
Give directions.	Label the line segments of the diagram you have drawn with the proper symbol, U, D, U_R, U_L, D_R, or D_L.	

Activity 5 *Launch*

TEACHER ACTION	TEACHER TALK	EXPECTED RESPONSE
Pass out Worksheet 5-1, Dot Paper Moves, and display a transparency of the Worksheet.	I am going to give you the code for a sequence of moves on the dot paper to trace this figure ____. Once we begin to draw, do not lift your pencil until we have finished the figure. Each time a direction is given it means to draw the specified line segment "from the point your pencil is on."	
Give directions slowly for drawing, or have students give directions starting from A.	Start with your pencil on Point A. Trace the figure as I give you the moves: Draw U_L, up to the left. From where you are, draw D_L, down to the left. Draw D, down. Draw D_R, down to the right. Draw U_R, up to the right.	
Explain.	Here is a set of moves that tells us how to draw a figure. Let's draw the figure together using these moves:	
Read the moves slowly and draw on the overhead.	U_R, U_R, U_R, D_R, D_L, D_L, D_R, D_L, U_L, U_L.	
Give directions. Students may want to cross out the moves as they draw them.	Do numbers 3, 4, 5, and 6 using the moves to draw the figures.	

Copyright © 1986 Addison-Wesley Publishing Company, Inc.

68

Activity 5 *Launch*

TEACHER ACTION	TEACHER TALK	EXPECTED RESPONSE
Pass out Worksheet 5-2, Copy the Figures, and cubes.	On the Copy the Figures worksheet there are pictures of six simple buildings. Build the first one on your desk. Position the building so that you see it as shown on the dot paper.	
Place a transparency of Worksheet 5-2 on the overhead, or draw figure 1 on a dot paper transparency.		
Start with any dot on the figure and talk the students around the figure. Have them trace over with a pencil or their fingers as the moves are given. One possible path: Start here → D_R, D, U_L, U, U_R, D_R, D, D_L, D_L, U, U_R, U_R.	For each problem on the page first build the building, position it as you see it on the dot paper, and then *copy* the figure exactly as it appears on the page. Do not add any extra lines. When you have difficulty, use the language of legal moves to talk yourself around a figure.	For students still having difficulties, use the language of moves to help a student reproduce the drawing by talking a student around the building; have students trace the figure or the actual building with their fingers, saying the moves to themselves or writing the moves on the figure.

TEACHER ACTION

As students finish, have them begin the Figures and Paths, Worksheet 5-3.

TEACHER TALK

In this activity you are asked to copy the figures, to count how many cubes are needed to build the figures, and to give a sequence of directions to travel from one point to another along the visible edges of the figure.

Build each building to check your answers to the questions.

EXPECTED RESPONSE

TEACHER ACTION	TEACHER TALK	EXPECTED RESPONSE
Discuss Worksheet 5-2.	How many blocks are needed to make each building?	1. 2 2. 8 3. 5 5. 5 6. 5
	What is the relationship between buildings C and D? What is the relationship between buildings E and F?	Same building, different views.
	Build C; turn it so you see it as it is in D.	
	Do the same for buildings E and F.	
	When isometric drawings have a lot of cubes, they can be difficult to read. One way to make them easier to see is to distinguish tops, left sides, and right sides.	
Demonstrate at the overhead on a drawing of one of the figures.	We will put stripes on tops and speckle the left-hand sides to help us read the drawings correctly.	
Discuss the answers to Figures and Paths, first concentrating on Paths and then on the number it takes to build each.	In giving directions for the edge, move from A to B. What is the shortest path we can give?	Many possible answers. 1. Moves: D_R, U_R, U_R, D_R, D_R, U_R. 2. Moves: U, D_L, U_L, U_L, U_L, D_L, D_R. 3. Moves: U, U_L, U, U, U_R, U_L.
In this discussion, be sure to make the point that the *length* of the shortest path is unique but that there may be several different shortest paths.		

Activity 5 *Summarize*

TEACHER ACTION	TEACHER TALK	EXPECTED RESPONSE
In exploring the longest path, let students propose a longest path and see if another student can find a longer one. Leave the question open for exploration.	If we do not allow the path to go over the same segment twice, what is the longest set of moves that will work?	Various answers.
	How many cubes does it take to build figure 1?	Six cubes are needed.
	How many cubes does it take to build figure 2?	Eight cubes are needed. If students answer 7, have them build the building to see that one cube is necessary that is not seen. It supports the tower.
	Are there any difficulties in counting the number of cubes needed to build the figure?	There may be hidden cubes.
	How many cubes are needed to build figure 3?	Seven, eight, or nine are correct; we could have the following mat plans
		Students who answer six have forgotten to support the tower with a cube.
		Have students build each of the correct answers and look to see that the extra cubes are hidden.

Isometric Dot Paper

Dot Paper Moves

1. Start at A. Give a series of dot paper moves that will produce the figure.

2. Start at B. Draw: U_R, U_R, U_R, D_R, D_L, D_L, D_R, D_L, U_L, U_L.

3. Start at C. Draw: U_R, U_R, U_L, U_R, D_R, D_R, D_R, D_L, U_L, D_L, D_L, U_L.

4. Start at D. Draw: U_L, U_R, U_L, U_L, D_L, D_R, D_L, U_L, D_L, D_R, D_R, U_R, D_R, U_R.

5. Start at E. Draw: U_R, U_R, D_R, D_R, D, D_L, D_L, U_L, U_L, U, D_R, D_R, U_R, U_R, D, D_L, D_L, U. (Part of the path is retraced.)

6. Start at F. Draw: U_L, D_L, D, D_L, D, D_L, D, D_R, U_R, U_R, U_R, U, U, U, D_L, D, D_L, D, D_L, D. Draw in the lines needed to show steps. Add lines to show each cube in the staircase.

Worksheet 5-1

Copy the Figures

Build each building from cubes. Copy each figure in the space provided. Copy the figures exactly as they appear.

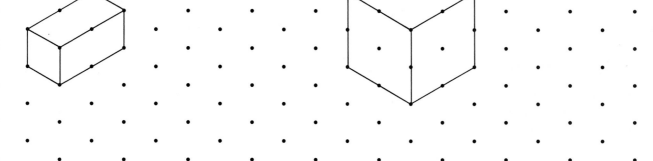

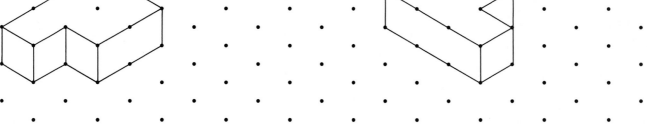

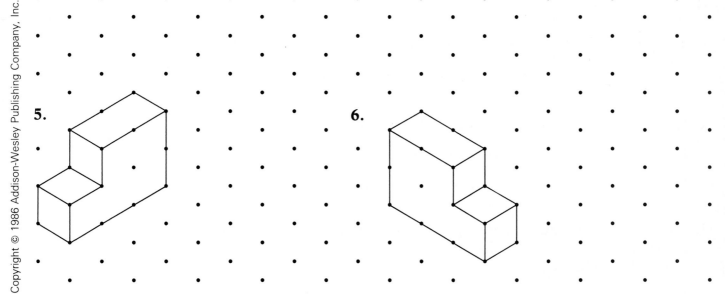

Figures and Paths

1. In the space provided, copy each figure exactly as it appears.

Figure 1

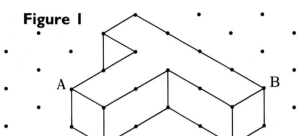

Figure 2

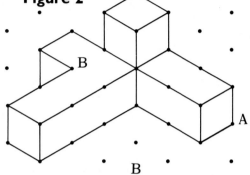

Figure 3

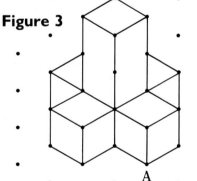

2. How many cubes would it take to build figure 1?

How many cubes would it take to build figure 2?

How many cubes would it take to build figure 3?

3. For each of the figures above give two different sets of dot paper moves (U_R, U, U_L, D_L, D, D_R) that will give a path from A to B along the visible edges of the building.

Figure 1 _____

Figure 2 _____

Figure 3 _____

Activity 6

LONGS, LETTERS, AND Ts

Copyright © 1986 Addison-Wesley Publishing Company, Inc.

OVERVIEW

Activity 6 explores the relationship between the physical properties of a cube and what is seen as the cube is turned to get an isometric view. Isometric dot paper allows drawings to be made of a building from any corner. Students learn to look at a building to see exactly what the dot paper shows. Consider the exposed cubes that are toward you; you can see a corner of the cube in the exact center of 6 other corners.

The symmetry of the object will influence how many different ways it can be drawn on the dot paper. The students are challenged to draw a three-long, three cubes stacked together, in every possible position. The long is less symmetric than a single cube. The result is that a three-long can be drawn in six different ways, while a single cube can be drawn in only two. An extension of this idea is to find out how many ways a capital T, made of a three-long with two cubes added, can be drawn. The students find that 24 different drawings can be made. While the students pursue these challenges they are constantly relating the solid object to their drawings and the drawings to the object. "Let's see, do I have this one already?" is a frequent comment.

The language of moves is used to analyze how to make three dimensional letters on the dot paper. This provides students with practice in drawing in a setting where their knowledge of what the letters look like provides perceptual help in determining if the drawing is correct.

Goals for students

1. Discover two different ways to draw a cube on the dot paper—top showing or bottom showing.
2. Discover how the isometric drawings of cubes are related to the properties of a cube.
   - The square face on the cube becomes a nonsquare rhombus on the dot paper.
   - The lengths of the edges are equal in both.
   - Parallel edges of the cube are parallel on the dot paper.
3. Learn to center a corner of a cube to see the dot paper picture in the solid object.
4. Discover different ways to draw the same object on the dot paper (three longs and Ts).
5. Become more proficient at making dot paper drawings and checking their accuracy.

Materials

Cubes.
Isometric Dot Paper (Materials 5-1).

Worksheets

*6-1, Drawing Longs.
*6-2, Three-Dimensional Letters.
 6-3, Drawing Ts.

Transparencies

Starred items should be made into transparencies.

TEACHER ACTION	TEACHER TALK	EXPECTED RESPONSE
Pass out Isometric Dot Paper (Materials 5-1), and cubes. Hold up a cube.	Name some characteristics of a cube. In other words, what makes a cube a cube?	Various answers; six faces, all squares; 12 edges, all of equal length; six corners.
	Look at a face of the cube. It is a square.	
	What are some properties of a square?	Four right angles, four equal sides, opposite sides are parallel.
Give directions.	On your dot paper, draw a picture of the *smallest cube* you can represent with a dot of the paper at each corner.	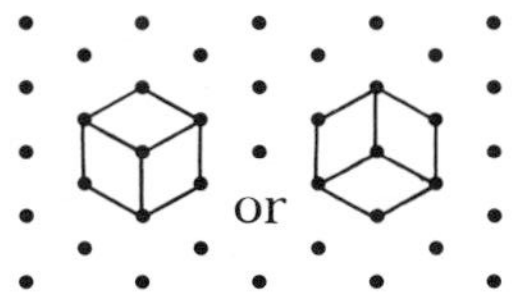
Collect answers. Copy a student's cube on the overhead *or* ask a student for a series of moves to draw one.	How should I hold the cube to match this picture of the cube?	Answer depends on cube drawn. Tip it so the top is showing or the bottom is showing.
Draw the other view of the cube on the overhead.	Did someone draw a different *view* of the cube?	Yes.
	We have found two different ways to show a cube on the dot paper. Draw both views on your dot paper.	
	Look at the cube you drew with the *top showing*. What shape is the top in the drawing?	Diamond (rhombus).
	Hold the cube tipped so that you see what your isometric picture shows.	If students have difficulty, suggest that they close one eye.
	What shape does the top appear to be?	Diamond (rhombus).
	Are all the faces of the cube the same shape in the drawing?	Yes, all diamonds.
	When you look at the cube itself, tipped as it appears on the dot paper, are the faces all the same shape and size?	Yes, all diamonds.

Activity 6 *Launch*

TEACHER ACTION	TEACHER TALK	EXPECTED RESPONSE
You may want to have students measure sides to see that they are equal. Have them measure the angles to find there are now two 60° angles and two 120° angles. Total is 60 + 60 + 120 + 120 = 360, the same as before.	What properties of the cube change when we represent it on the dot paper?	Angles are not 90°.
	What properties remain the same?	Parallel sides are still parallel. Faces are still congruent. Edges are still the same length.
	When you look at your cube as it is shown on the dot paper, where is the front corner of the cube?	In the center of the six other corners.
	Where is the front corner of the cube in your drawing?	In the center of the drawing or in the center of a hexagon.
	This tells you how to look at a cube and to draw it on the dot paper. Make sure that you tip the cube so that the front corner is in the center.	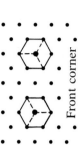 Front corner
Explain and draw.	One way to draw a cube is to draw a hexagon (six-sided figure). Find the center dot and make either a ⅄ to have the top showing or a Y to have the bottom showing.	

TEACHER ACTION	TEACHER TALK	EXPECTED RESPONSE
Explain.	Another way to draw a cube is to start with a picture of a square, or a diamond.	
Draw ◇ on the overhead.	Draw a diamond like this on your dot paper. This isometric square can be the top of a cube or the bottom of a cube.	
Draw on the overhead.	Look at your cube. If this is the top, three parallel lines go down. Draw them.	
Give directions.	Draw another isometric square and make it the bottom of a cube.	
Explain.	Vertical parallel lines on the dot paper show height. Slanted parallel lines on the dot paper show depth.	
Make sure cubes are available. Pass out a sheet of dot paper.		
Hold up three cubes places together.	This is a three-long. It can be drawn on the dot paper in several positions. Make a three-long and turn it to look at different corners: up, slanted to the left, and so on.	
Give directions. Allow time for students to draw. Check to see that students are using the dot paper in this position ▢ . (The figures are harder to orient on dot paper turned sideways.)	Draw every different view of a three-long you can find.	
	How many views of the three-long did you get?	
Give directions.	As a summary let's carefully develop a scheme for getting all possible views of a long.	Students will eventually find six views.

Activity 6 *Launch*

TEACHER ACTION	TEACHER TALK	EXPECTED RESPONSE
Draw a cube on the overhead.	We can make a three-long by adding two cubes on to a single cube. Can we do this on the dot paper?	
As you go through this, use an overhead and a transparency of dot paper to provide immediate feedback.	Where can you add cubes without having to erase any lines?	
	Draw down; up and to the right; up and to the left (D, U_R, U_L).	
	Let's add these and we will see that we have three of the views of a three-long.	
	Let's do the same thing with a cube tipped so that we can see the bottom.	
	Now, where can we add cubes?	
	Draw up; down and to the right; down and to the left (U, D_R, D_L).	
	This gets all six of the views.	

TEACHER ACTION	TEACHER TALK	EXPECTED RESPONSE

Explain.

Another useful way to draw a three-long is to first draw a parallelogram that is three-long.

Then we can thicken the parallelogram in two ways to form a three-long. In this case we can draw up and to the right, U_R, or down and to the left, D_L.

We can rotate this same parallelogram and draw it in two other positions. Each of the basic three parallelograms can be thickened in two ways. We get the six different longs again. Notice that we use each of the six basic moves on the dot paper in this scheme.

With figure 1 we use U_R and D_L.

With figure 2 we use U_L and D_R.

With figure 3 we use U and D.

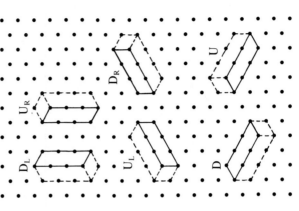

Pass out Worksheet 6-1, Drawing Longs.

On Worksheet 6-1 draw each family of three-longs, first by adding on to cubes; second by thickening parallelograms.

Activity 6 *Launch*

TEACHER ACTION	TEACHER TALK	EXPECTED RESPONSE
Pass out Isometric Dot Paper and Worksheet 6-2, Three-Dimensional Letters.	On your paper draw two Ls like this.	
	Thicken the right-hand L by drawing U_R lines from every corner possible without drawing inside the original letter.	
	Connect these corner lines. Shade the thickened part.	
	On the left L, thicken by drawing down to the left, D_L. Connect and shade.	
	Build an L from four cubes and look at it in both of these positions.	
	Now draw two Ls like this.	
	From the upper right corner, what slant lines can I draw that do not intersect the figure?	U_L or D_R.
	Thicken your Ls one in each of these ways, U_L and D_R.	
	If I try to draw U or D from a corner of either L what happens?	You either hit the figure or make the L longer.
	To make letters look 3-D we have found four ways to thicken them. Worksheet 6-2, Three-Dimensional Letters, gives you practice in each of these four ways.	

Activity 6 *Explore*

TEACHER ACTION

As students finish, pose the challenge. Pass out Worksheet 6-3, Drawing Ts.

It helps to tape five cubes together temporarily.

Some students will be able to draw all 24 or figure out that there *are* 24 possibilities. Other students will be frustrated if pushed to draw all 24. Drawing one complete family (see summary) is a reasonable goal to expect of *all* students.

TEACHER TALK

Add two cubes to a three-long to make a T. Tape these together so that we can freely turn the T in space. In how many different positions can we draw the T on the dot paper?

Try to answer this question by drawing Ts on your paper. As you draw, try to find an explanation of how many there must be.

EXPECTED RESPONSE

Students can be helped to find additional Ts by being reminded of the mirror line idea from Activity 1. Below are two examples using a vertical and then a horizontal mirror line to create a different T.

mirror line

mirror line

Activity 6 *Summarize*

TEACHER ACTION	TEACHER TALK	EXPECTED RESPONSE
The summary for the Ts should come only after the students have worked on the problem enough to see that there are many possibilities.		
Ask.	How many different Ts do you think can be drawn on the dot paper?	There are 24 views. These 24 can be found by taking the six longs and adding two cubes on each of the ends in the two possible positions. Each of the six generates four different Ts.
	Is this problem related to the three-long problem?	
	How many ways can you add two cubes to a three-long to get a T?	
Display students' Ts on the bulletin board.		
You may want to display a three-long with a cube added in the center—both the solid object and a picture—on the overhead.	Try your thinking on this new problem.	
	How many ways can you draw this solid on the dot paper?	24, because you can make four from each of six longs.
Display a three-long with two cubes added as shown—both the solid and the picture.	How many ways can you draw this solid on the dot paper?	24; same reasoning.
	And this one?	48, because you can make eight from each of six longs.

85

TEACHER ACTION

TEACHER TALK

Here is a family of Ls drawn from the same basic three-long.

EXPECTED RESPONSE

Drawing Longs

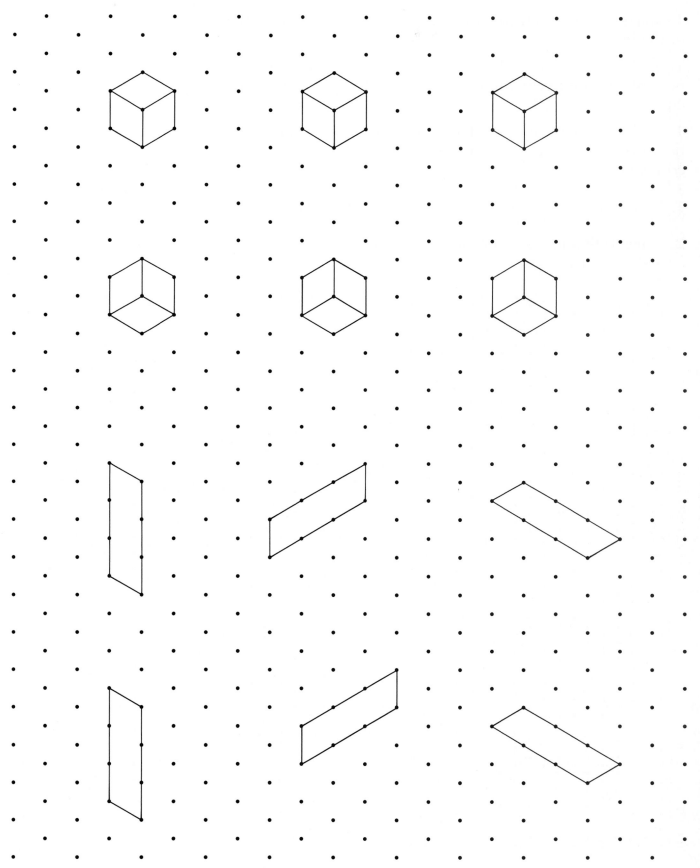

Three-Dimensional Letters

To make three-dimensional letters on dot paper, first draw the front of the letter.

To make the top of the letter show, draw U_R from every corner possible without drawing inside the original letter. Then connect the corner lines.

To make the bottom of the letter show, draw D_L from every corner possible without drawing inside the original letter. Then connect the corner lines.

1. Make the top show on CUBIC and the bottom show on FACT.

2. Make TOP and CUP look 3-D in different ways. You will have to use U_L and D_R moves.

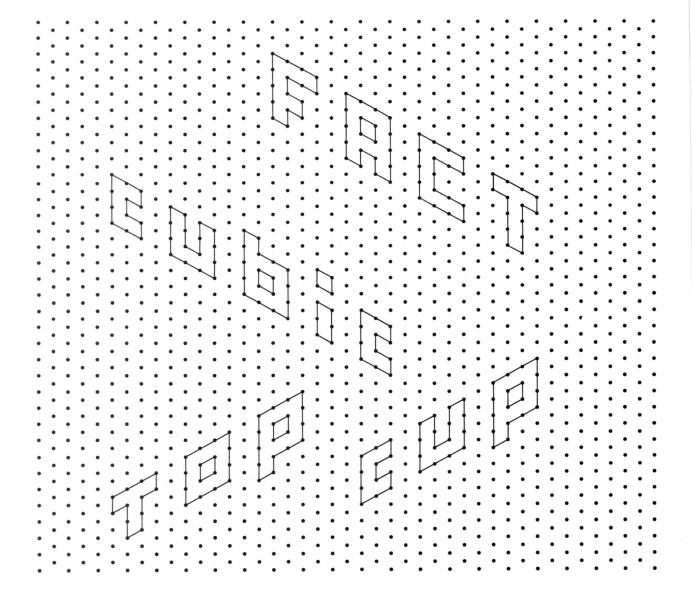

Worksheet 6-2

Drawing Ts

Make a capital T from five cubes. Pretend it is glued together so that you can turn it freely, even upside down, and look at it from every corner. How many *different* ways can you draw the T on the dot paper? An example is given.

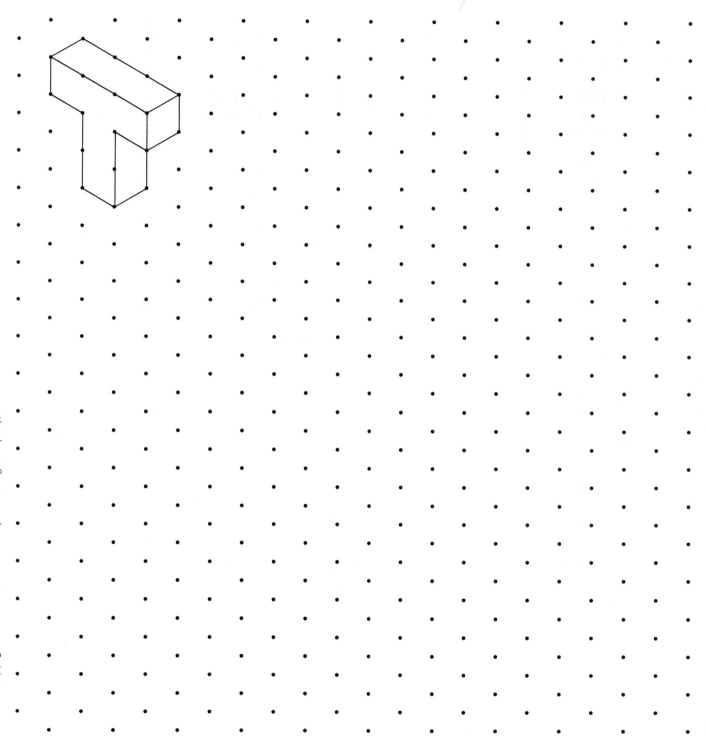

SEEING THE ISOMETRIC VIEW

Copyright © 1986 Addison-Wesley Publishing Company, Inc.

OVERVIEW

This activity provides a change of pace and direction. Students have been working with the isometric dot paper; now they will learn to look at a building from a corner and see the building as it can be drawn on the isometric dot paper. It takes practice to look at buildings and be able to see the isometric view.

After the introductory study of the four corner views of building BB, students match corners and buildings to 12 isometric drawings. This matching requires a great deal of eye movement back and forth from buildings to drawings. Once these views have been matched, students are asked to draw the isometric views of a simple building.

Adding and Removing Cubes (Worksheet 7-3) has students look at a drawing, build from the drawing, add or remove a cube, then draw the modified building. Again the emphasis is on going back and forth visually from a building to a picture.

Goals for students

1. Match visually an isometric drawing to the corner of a building from which it was made.
2. Learn to draw isometric views of a simple building.

Materials

Cubes.
Mats AA–EE (Materials 1-10 to 1-12).

Worksheets

*7-1, Corner Views.
7-2, Matching Isometric Drawings.
7-3, Adding and Removing Cubes.

Transparencies

Starred item should be made into a transparency.

SEEING THE ISOMETRIC VIEW

TEACHER ACTION	TEACHER TALK	EXPECTED RESPONSE
Pass out cubes; Mats AA–EE, (Materials 1-10 to 1-12); Worksheet 7-1, Corner Views; Worksheet 7-2, Matching Isometric Views; and Worksheet 7-3, Adding and Removing Cubes.	Take out the mat for BB and build the building on your mat labeled FRONT, BACK, LEFT, RIGHT (Worksheet 1-1).	
Review how to look at a cube.	We are going to look at this building from different corners.	
	Turn the mat so that you are looking at the building from the corner where the left and front sides meet.	
	Adjust your eye level so that the foremost corner of the top cube is in the middle of the cube.	
Display the top half of Worksheet 7-1, Corner Views, on the overhead.	Now look at Worksheet 7-1, Corner Views. Which of the views of building BB is what you see?	D.
Record on the transparency.	Label the corner of the mat.	
	Look at each of the other views and label the corner of the mat from which the view was drawn.	
Define.	These corner views are called *isometric views.*	

Activity 7 *Launch*

TEACHER ACTION	TEACHER TALK	EXPECTED RESPONSE
Explain.	Now, work in groups and build AA, DD, EE (dismantle BB).	
	Each of the 12 pictures on Worksheet 7-2, Matching Isometric Views, is a corner view of one of the three buildings. Identify the building and label the corner of the mat in each picture.	

Activity 7 *Explore*

TEACHER ACTION	TEACHER TALK	EXPECTED RESPONSE
Explain.	On the lower half of Worksheet 7-1, Corner Views, is the mat plan of a five-cube building. Build it on your mat.	
	Draw all four corner views. In each view include a corner of the mat labeled with the names of the sides you see.	
As students finish, have them do Worksheet 7-3, Adding and Removing Cubes.		
Early finishers may be given a clean sheet of dot paper and four cubes taped together to form an L. Have them draw as many views of the L as possible.		
Ask.	How many views of the L do you think there are?	48.
(This was discussed in the summary of Activity 6.)		

93

Corner Views

Here are four views of building BB. Label the corner of the mat
with the names of the visible sides of the building: FRONT, RIGHT,
BACK, LEFT.

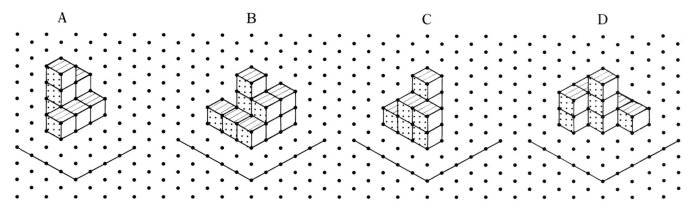

A   B   C   D

Do this part *after* you have completed Worksheet 7-2, Matching
Isometric Views. Build and draw the four corner views of this
building. Include a corner of the mat labeled with the names of the
visible sides.

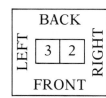

Matching Isometric Views

Build buildings AA, DD, and EE on the mat plans provided. Each of the buildings is drawn below from each of its corners. The corners are the FRONT LEFT, FRONT RIGHT, BACK LEFT, or BACK RIGHT. Match the building and its corner to the correct drawing. Indicate which corner the building is viewed from by writing in FRONT, RIGHT, BACK, or LEFT.

1. Building _____

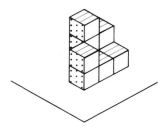

2. Building _____

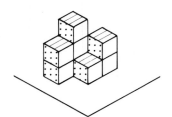

3. Building _____

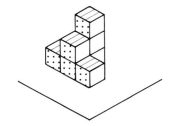

4. Building _____

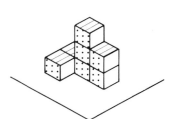

5. Building _____

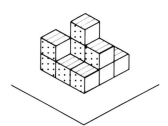

6. Building _____

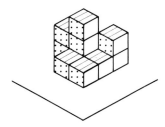

7. Building _____

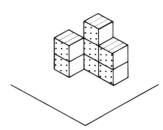

8. Building _____

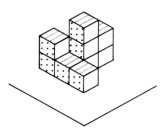

9. Building _____

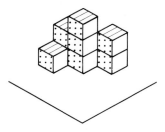

10. Building _____

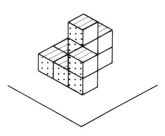

11. Building _____

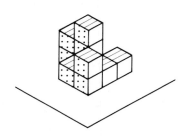

12. Building _____

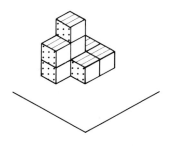

Adding and Removing Cubes

Build each building with cubes. Take away the shaded cube or cubes and draw what remains.

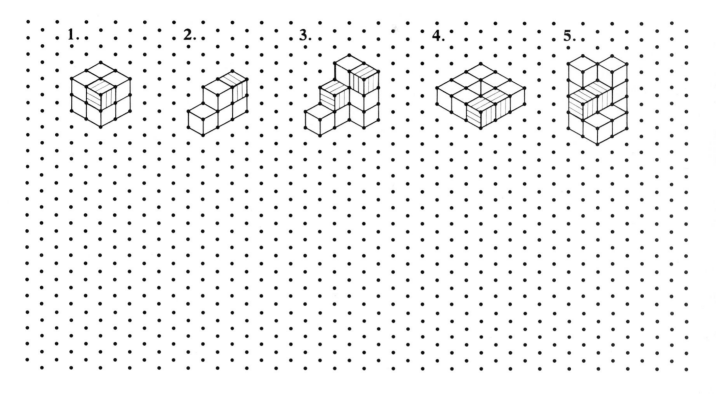

Build each building. Then add a cube to each shaded face and draw the new building.

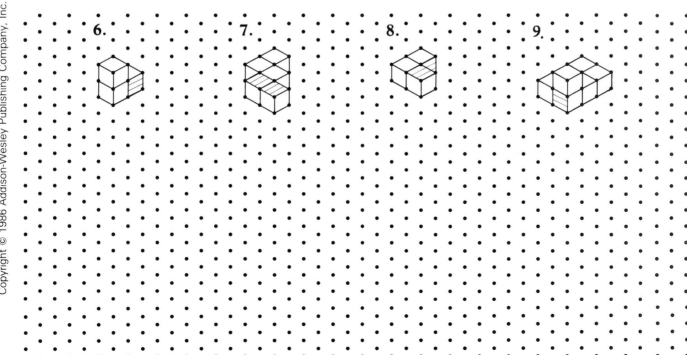

LOOKING AT BUILDINGS AND VIEWS

OVERVIEW

This activity provides a reminder of the first scheme that was used to represent buildings. The question of uniqueness is raised again. The major focus is on building and observing rather than making drawings.

The students are asked to return to the first scheme and draw a set of plans from an isometric drawing. This relates the plans and calls for visualizing the flat views from an isometric drawing. Students then look again at the isometric drawing and draw plans for other possible buildings made from that drawing.

Practice in carefully looking at buildings is provided by the Hidden Cubes and Uniqueness worksheets. Students explore, for example, exactly what can be hidden by a stack of three cubes. Then they explore the question of whether or not a building is uniquely determined by two isometric views.

Goals for students

1. Learn to make a set of plans from isometric drawings.
2. Build from an isometric drawing.
3. Discover possible hidden cubes in isometric drawings.
4. Discover that two isometric drawings of a building do not necessarily make a unique building.

Materials

Cubes.

Worksheets

*8-1, Camera Views.
8-2, Hidden Cubes.
8-3, Uniqueness.
8-4, Adding and Removing Cubes II (optional).

Transparencies

Starred item should be made into a transparency.

LOOKING AT BUILDINGS AND VIEWS

TEACHER ACTION	TEACHER TALK	EXPECTED RESPONSE
Pass out cubes, building mat (Worksheet 1-1); and Worksheet 8-1, Camera Views. Display a transparency of Worksheet 8-1, Camera Views.	We're going to begin by using the set of plans again. Build the building and make a set of plans. Assume that you can see part of every cube.	
Draw outline of the base on the overhead.	Let's make a mat plan of the building.	Some students will draw the base sideways.
Fill in mat plan.	Turn your building so that you are looking at it from the front right corner.	
	Place a cube where I've made an X on the mat plan. Can you see it?	No, it is hidden.
Record new base.	Can we put another cube on the X?	No.
Record answers until this base has been found.	Where else can a cube be?	Various answers.
	To check whether a cube is hidden, look at the building so that the front corner of the blocking cube is in the middle.	
	Draw the front and side views of this building.	

100

Activity 8 *Explore*

TEACHER ACTION	TEACHER TALK	EXPECTED RESPONSE
Pass out cubes; Worksheet 8-2, Hidden Cubes; and Worksheet 8-3, Uniqueness.	This activity is about hidden cubes, maximal and minimal.	
Remind students of how to look at a cube and how to check for hidden cubes.	Before starting, look at a cube from the top. Hold it so you see exactly the isometric view.	
As students explore, help those who are having difficulty to learn to look at the building (with one eye closed if necessary) so that what they see is exactly what is drawn on the isometric dot paper. Remind them of how to look at the building to check for hidden cubes.	Where is the front corner?	In the center of the hexagon.
Pass out Worksheet 8-4, Adding and Removing Cubes II, to early finishers, or assign it as homework.		

Activity 8 *Summarize*

TEACHER ACTION	TEACHER TALK	EXPECTED RESPONSE
Collect responses to Worksheets 8-2 and 8-3, Hidden Cubes and Uniqueness.	What can we say about maximal and minimal buildings in isometric drawings?	Buildings aren't always unique; there is more than one way to build them.
	How can we hide blocks?	On the base in back of stacks or on layers behind stacks.

Camera Views

Build this building with cubes. Assume that you can see at least part of every cube.

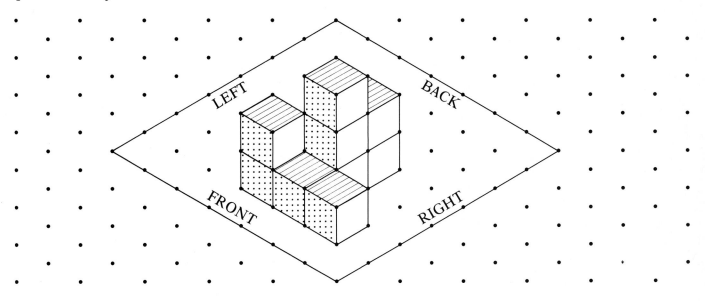

Make a set of plans.

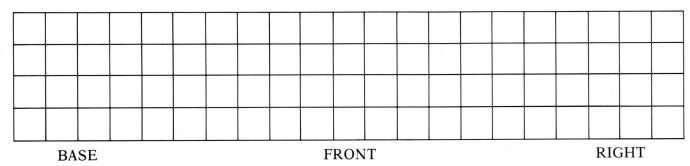

BASE   FRONT   RIGHT

Now assume there are some hidden cubes. Add as many cubes as you can, but make sure the **FRONT RIGHT** view is the same as in the picture. Make a set of plans for your new building.

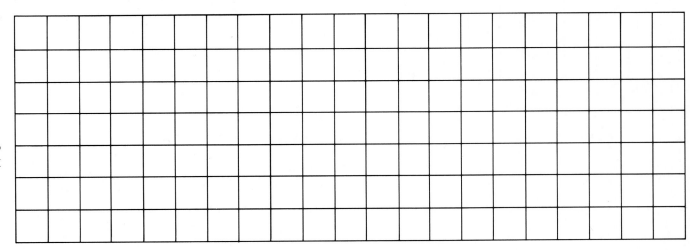

Hidden Cubes

1. Find several different buildings that have this FRONT LEFT view. Make a mat plan for each one.

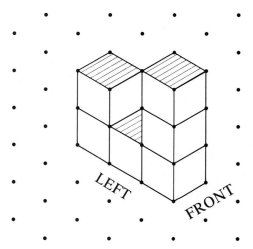

2. Find minimal and maximal buildings that have this FRONT RIGHT view. Draw mat plans for each. (Check your orientation.)

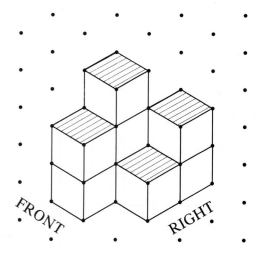

Worksheet 8-2

Uniqueness

In each problem below you are given two corner views of the same building. Build a building with these views. Draw a mat plan for a building that could have these views.

1.

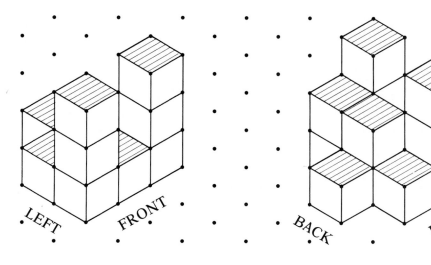

2.

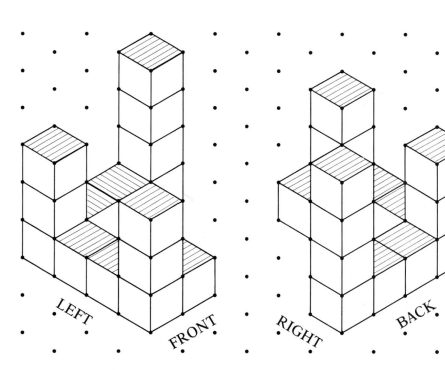

Adding and Removing Cubes II

Build each building. Then add a cube to each shaded face and draw
the new building.

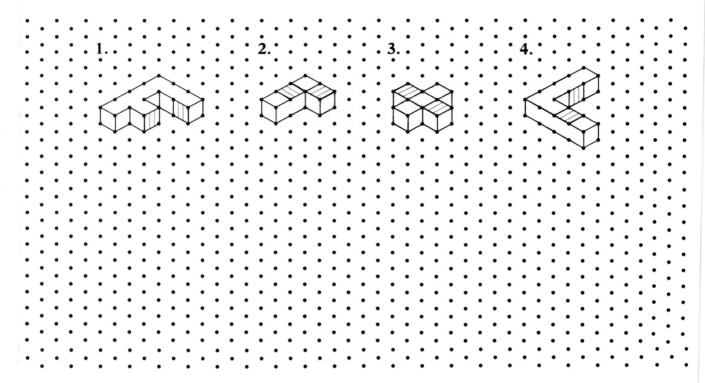

1.　　　2.　　　3.　　　4.

If you try to remove the cubes in these buildings, the buildings will
collapse. Pretend the remaining cubes are glued together and draw
what is left when the shaded cubes are removed.

5. 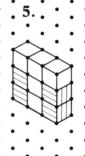　　6. 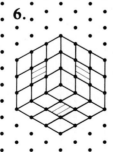　　7. 　　8.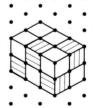

Worksheet 8-4

Activity 9

TWO-PIECE PUZZLE

OVERVIEW

This activity differs slightly from some of the visualization tasks undertaken in prior activities. In this activity two simple buildings, called puzzle pieces, are put together to match a drawing of a building made from the two pieces. Students are asked to shade the drawing to show each puzzle piece. To be successful, students must put the pieces together not only in the right combination but also with the correct orientation. This task further enhances the students' ability to read information from a two-dimensional drawing of a solid.

Little is needed in the way of a launch or summary. Students enjoy this activity *very much!*

Goals for students

1. Practice building and drawing.
2. Examine pictures of buildings for specific information.

Materials

Cubes.

Worksheets

9-1, Two-Piece Puzzle I.
9-2, Two-Piece Puzzle II.

TWO-PIECE PUZZLE

TEACHER ACTION

The activity is much more interesting if the cubes are temporarily taped together to make a solid. Ordinary transparent tape works well on plastic cubes. Be sure to make the two puzzle pieces of different colors so that the students can clearly see where they are in the combined solid.

Students need the two puzzle pieces made from four blocks each and Worksheet 9-1, Two-Puzzle Pieces I.

Hold up the two puzzle pieces. Tell students to put them together to make Building I.

Explain the purpose of shading one piece to show how the building was put together.

Note: These puzzle pieces are part of the "soma cube," a commercial puzzle. Some students may have seen it or you may have it in your Math lab.

TEACHER TALK

Today we are going to look at and build buildings that are made from two separate buildings, similar to 3-D puzzles.

Notice how we need only to shade in one of the puzzle pieces to show how the building was made from the two puzzle pieces.

Build the other buildings from the two puzzle pieces. Shade one of the pieces in each drawing.

EXPECTED RESPONSE

Activity 9 *Explore*

TEACHER ACTION

As students finish, pass out Worksheet 9-2, Two-Piece Puzzle II.

As an extra challenge, you may want to have students create two *different* puzzle pieces and then *build* and draw buildings made from the new pieces. Or have students make a building and draw it using three puzzle pieces from Worksheet 9-1 and Worksheet 9-2.

TEACHER TALK

EXPECTED RESPONSE

Two-Piece Puzzle I

Use the two puzzle pieces to build each building. Show how you
built them by shading in one of the puzzle pieces on each drawing.

Puzzle Pieces

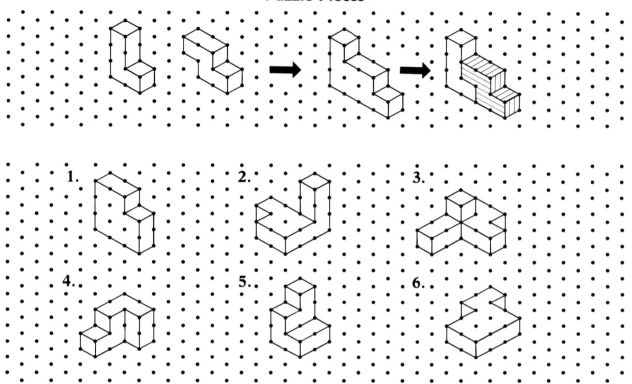

1.

2.

3.

4.

5.

6.

Find *three* different ways to make a building from the puzzle pieces.
Make a drawing of each of your buildings.

Two-Piece Puzzle II

In each part use the puzzle pieces to build each building. Show how you built them by shading in one of the puzzle pieces on each drawing.

Puzzle Pieces

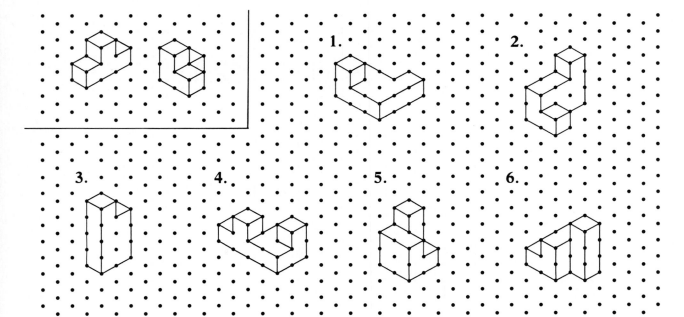

Puzzle Pieces

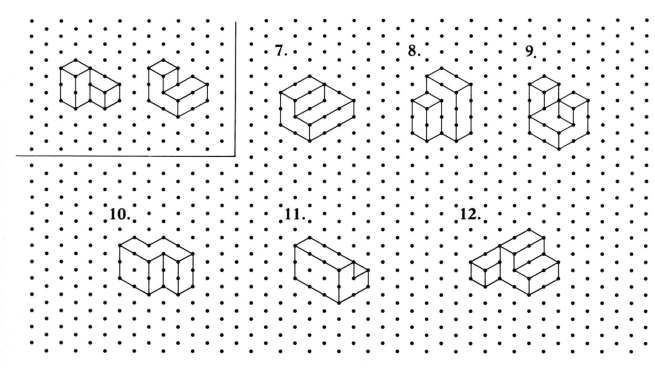

Activity 10

VISUALIZATION AND ORIENTATION— A SUMMARY

OVERVIEW

After practice on a simple building, a summary of the unit is provided by giving another building in Mat Plan form: Students are asked to produce a set of plans and the four isometric corner views of the building. This encourages a review of much that has been studied. Differences and similarities between the two schemes can be seen. The opposite views in isometric drawings are *not* mirror images. However, both schemes may have hidden cubes; a maximal building is still unique.

Drawing single-layer buildings with stretched-out designs provides an extra challenge for the more advanced students.

As a final step, the archeologist's mystery building used to launch the unit is built, and an extra challenge to produce an isometric view of the building is given to those students who want to try it.

Goals for students

1. Learn to draw isometric views of simple buildings from a mat plan.
2. Use both schemes to represent a building in eight views (FRONT, BACK, RIGHT, LEFT, and the four corner views).
3. Discover differences and similarities between the two schemes for representing buildings.
4. Build the archeologist's mystery building.

Materials

Cubes.

Isometric Dot Paper (Materials 5-1).

Worksheets

10-1, Four Views.
*10-2, Drawing Single-Layer Buildings.
10-3, Eight Ways.
10-4, The Archeologist's Exploration.
10-5, The Archeologist's Exploration (continued).

Transparencies

Starred items should be made into transparencies.

VISUALIZATION AND ORIENTATION—
A SUMMARY

TEACHER ACTION

Pass out Worksheet 10-1, Four Views, and cubes.

Give directions.

As an extra challenge, have students build an enlargement of building JJ so that each dimension is two times as big. Draw one view on dot paper.

Worksheet 10-2, Drawing Single-Layer Buildings, can be used as an extra challenge for early finishing students or as a class activity. If you use it as a class activity, the following quick launch will be helpful to the students.

Put a transparency of Worksheet 10-2, Drawing Single-Layer Buildings, on the overhead.

Give directions.

TEACHER TALK

A mat plan for building JJ is given on Worksheet 10-1. Build JJ on your building mat.

Now turn JJ to a corner and draw an isometric view from that corner. Label the drawing by the corner from which it was drawn.

Do this for each of the four corners.

How many cubes does it take to build the enlargement of JJ?

Build this building on your mat.

Turn it so you are looking at the building from the FRONT LEFT corner.

EXPECTED RESPONSE

JJ enlarged takes 40 cubes. $5 \times 2^3 = 40$.

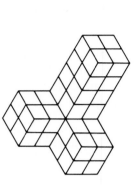

If students have difficulty, the strategy of drawing the top first and then thickening is helpful.

Activity 10 *Explore*

TEACHER ACTION	TEACHER TALK	EXPECTED RESPONSE
Draw the FRONT LEFT view on the overhead.	We are going to draw the FRONT LEFT view.	
	Do the same for buildings 1, 2, and 3. Building 1 is started for you.	
As an extra challenge, have students draw views from each of the four corners.		
Pass out Worksheet 10-3, Eight Ways.	We are going to summarize all that we have done in this unit by representing a building using both schemes. Build building KK and draw it from four views—FRONT, BACK, RIGHT, LEFT—and from four corners.	
Give directions.		

LEFT

FRONT

Activity 10 *Summarize*

TEACHER ACTION

As an extra challenge, have students draw eight views of building LL below.

Put students into groups of three or four and have them build the mystery building from The Archeologist's Exploration (Worksheets 10-4 and 10-5). They should make a mat plan of the maximal building on the outline of the base that was given.

For an extra challenge, have students draw an isometric view of the mystery building from Activity 1. Suggest that they draw the building from the FRONT RIGHT corner and start on the extreme edge of a sheet of dot paper. To continue the story line of Activity 1, this drawing could be done to leave to future generations as additional evidence of how the building looked when it was originally constructed.

EXPECTED RESPONSE

116

Activity 10 *Summarize*

TEACHER ACTION	TEACHER TALK	EXPECTED RESPONSE
Check answers to Worksheet 10-1, Four Views, and Worksheet 10-3, Eight Ways.	When I stand in FRONT of a building and you stand in BACK of the same building, how do our views compare?	They are mirror images.
	If I make an isometric drawing from a corner of a building and you stand opposite me and make a drawing from the opposite corner, are the drawings mirror images?	No.
	Can you think of other ways in which the two schemes to represent a building are different?	Various answers.
	How are they similar?	It is easier to visualize in the isometric drawing; neither gives a unique building.
	Which seems to give more information, a set of three drawings—BASE, FRONT, LEFT, or one isometric drawing? What if you have two isometric drawings?	It is easier to construct a building from the BASE, FRONT, and LEFT than from one isometric drawing.
		With two isometric drawings you can figure out what the base is.
		Isometric views are from corners.
		It is easier to read information from isometric views, such as the two-piece puzzles.
Check mat plans of the archeologist's mystery building on Worksheets 10-4 and 10-5, and show any drawings that students make.		

Four Views

Build the following building and draw the view from each corner on isometric dot paper. Label each view by the corner from which it is drawn.

Building JJ

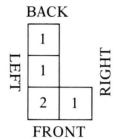

Drawing Single-Layer Buildings

Below is a mat plan for a building and an isometric drawing of the same building. It is the view of the building from the FRONT LEFT corner.

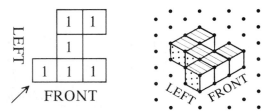

Each of these is a mat plan for a building. Build each building. Make an isometric drawing of the building as it looks from the FRONT LEFT corner.

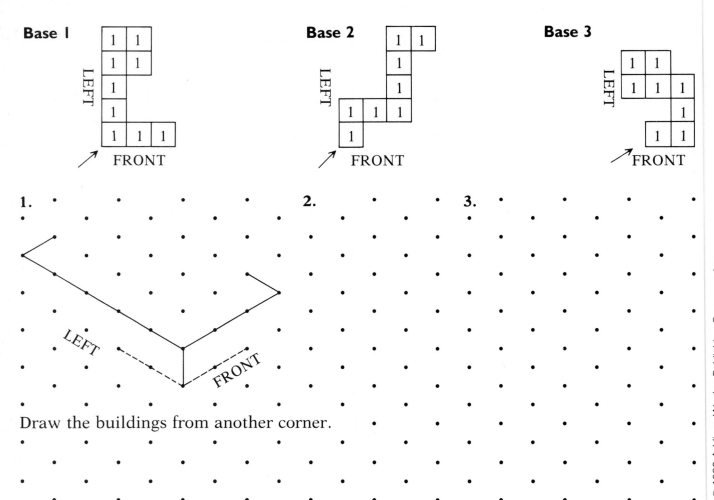

Base 1

Base 2

Base 3

1.

2.

3.

Draw the buildings from another corner.

Eight Ways

You have learned different ways to draw a building and to give information about the building.

There is the architectural way, which draws views of a building from the FRONT, RIGHT and we could add, BACK and LEFT.

Then there is the isometric way, which can show a building from any of its four corners.

Here is a mat plan for a building KK.

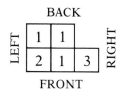

Draw the four architectural views of the building and the four isometric views of the building.

The Archeologist's Explorations

An archeologist exploring a small isolated island has found the ruins of an ancient building. The mystery building had been made from large cubes of stone cut from the island quarry. The stones are scattered around the immediate area of the foundation of the building. The terrain and remoteness of the island suggest that no stones have been removed from the area.

There is a clear outline of the foundation of the building left in the ground.

Outline of the Base of the Archeologist's Mystery Building

Worksheet 10-4

The Archeologist's Explorations (continued)

An experimental area is excavated between the wings of the foundation. Among the pots unearthed are several ceremonial pots and plates with square, geometric designs. They appear to belong with the building. In the past archeologists have found that the designs on such ceremonial pots are often pictorial records of the times.

On several of the plates the designs are the same. The archeologist believes that the designs on the plates are views of the building that once stood on the foundation. Here are the designs. Can you reconstruct the archeologist's mystery building?

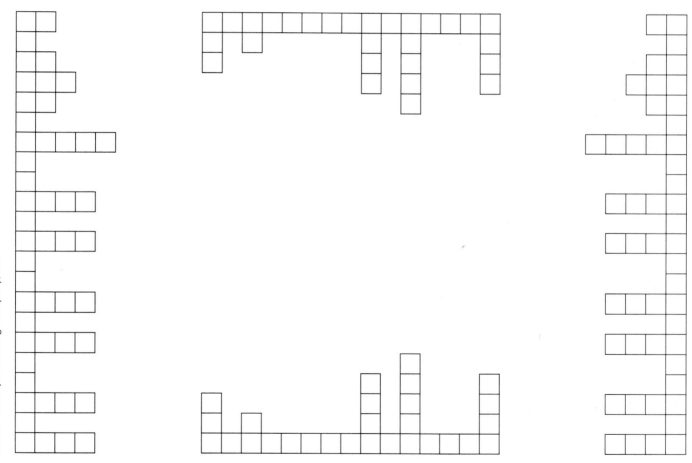

Review Problems

1. Picture the building that the mat plan at the right describes.

FRONT

   a) Which of the views below is the view of the building from the front? _____

   b) Which of the views below is the view of the building from the right? _____

A

B

C

D

E

2. Complete the drawings to show what will appear if a mirror is set on the dividing line.

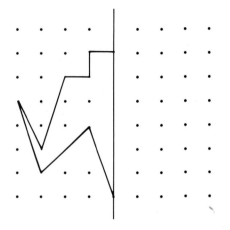

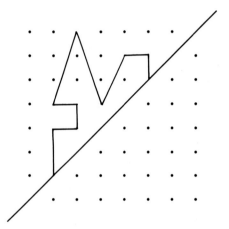

3. Draw a set of plans—BASE, FRONT, RIGHT—for the building given in the mat plan at the right.

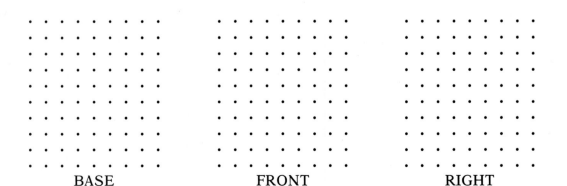

BASE   FRONT   RIGHT

Review Problems, page 1

Review Problems

4. Picture a building that has the FRONT and RIGHT views shown below. Draw its BASE. Then number the squares in the BASE to create a mat plan for the building.

BASE

FRONT   RIGHT

5. Picture a building that has the set of plans shown below. On the BASE record a mat plan for the building.

BASE   FRONT   RIGHT

6. a) How many cubes are needed to construct a minimal building for the plans given below? _____

   b) How many cubes are needed to construct a maximal building for the plans given below? _____

BASE   FRONT   RIGHT

7. How many different views of the shape below can be drawn on isometric dot paper if the shape can be turned freely? _____

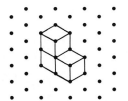

Review Problems

8. Draw the isometric view from the **BACK RIGHT** corner of the building given in the mat plan below.

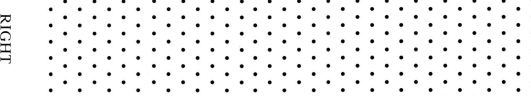

BACK

LEFT

1		
2	1	
3	2	1

RIGHT

FRONT

9. Draw the building that would remain if the shaded cubes were removed.

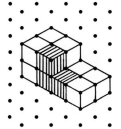

10. a) What is the maximum number of cubes that the given building below could be built out of? _____

b) What is the minimum number of cubes that the building below could be built out of? _____

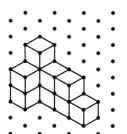

11. Which drawing shows another view of the first building? _____

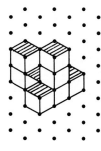 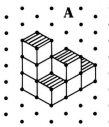 A 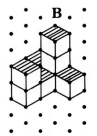 B 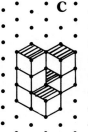 C 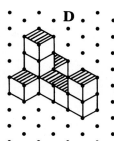 D  E

Review Problems

12. Which of the following is *not* a corner view of the building given in the mat plan?

FRONT

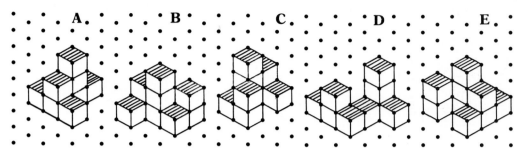

13. Which of the buildings can be made from the two pieces given?

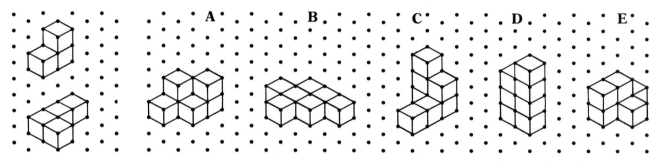

14. Which drawing shows the view from the FRONT LEFT corner?

FRONT

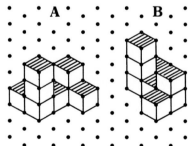
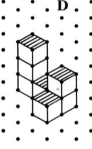
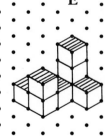

15. You are given the BASE, FRONT, and RIGHT view of a building. Which mat plan that can be completed to fit the building?

BASE   FRONT   RIGHT

Review Problems, page 4

Unit Test

Answer the sample questions and then wait for further instructions.

This is an example of the mat plan of a building. The number in each square tells how many cubes are to be placed on that square.

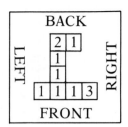

Use the information in the mat plan to answer the two sample questions.

Sample 1

This is a corner view of the building above. Which corner was it drawn from?

A FRONT RIGHT

B BACK RIGHT

C BACK LEFT

D FRONT LEFT

Sample 2

These are the views of the *same* building when looked at straight on from the sides. Which is the FRONT view?

STOP.
Wait until you are told to continue.

Unit Test, page 1

Unit Test

1. You are given a picture of a building drawn from the FRONT RIGHT corner. Find the BACK view.

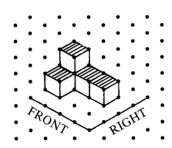

A B C D E

2. You are given a picture of a building drawn from the FRONT RIGHT corner. Find the RIGHT view.

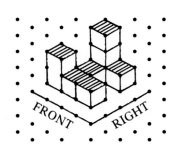

A B C D E

3. You are given the mat plan of a building. Find the LEFT view.

FRONT

A B C D E

4. You are given the RIGHT view of a building. Find the LEFT view.

RIGHT

A B C D E

Unit Test

5. You are given the BACK view of a building. Find the FRONT view.

	A	B	C	D	E

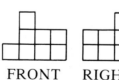

BACK

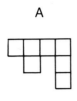

6. You are given the BASE, FRONT view, and RIGHT view of a building. Find the mat plan that can be completed to fit the building.

BASE   FRONT   RIGHT

A   B   C   D   E

7. You are given the BASE, FRONT view, and RIGHT view of a building. Find the mat plan for the building that uses the greatest number of cubes and also fits the given base and views.

BASE   FRONT   RIGHT

A   B   C   D   E

Unit Test

8. You are given the BASE and FRONT view of a building. Which of the views could *not* be a LEFT view of the building?

BASE   FRONT

A   B   C   D   E

9. Find the view from the FRONT LEFT corner.

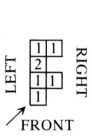

A    B 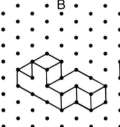   C    D 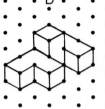   E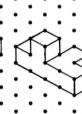

10. You are given the mat plan of a building. Find the view from the BACK LEFT corner.

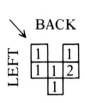

A    B    C    D    E

11. You are given two puzzle pieces. Which of these buildings can be made from the two pieces?

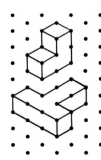

A    B    C 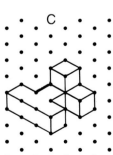   D    E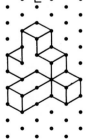

Unit Test

12. You are given one view of a building. Find another view of the building.

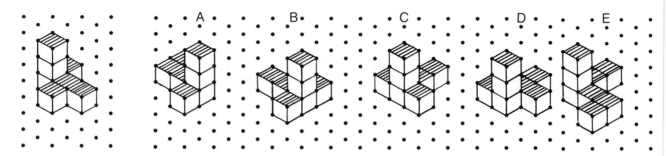

13. You are given one view of a building. Find another view of the building.

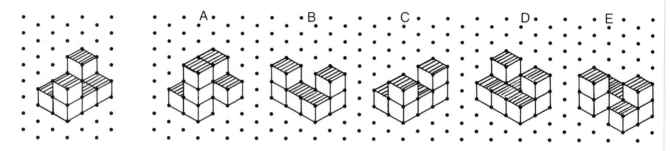

14. You are given a mat plan for a building. Which of the following is *not* a corner view of the building?

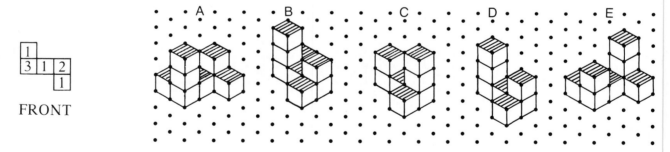

15. You are given an isometric drawing of a corner view of a building. What is the *maximum* number of cubes that could be used to build it?

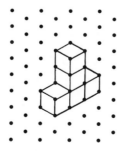

A	B	C	D	E
5	6	7	8	9

Unit Test, page 5

Unit Test Answer Sheet

Sample 1	A	B	C	D
Sample 2	A	B	C	D

1.	A	B	C	D	E
2.	A	B	C	D	E
3.	A	B	C	D	E
4.	A	B	C	D	E
5.	A	B	C	D	E
6.	A	B	C	D	E
7.	A	B	C	D	E
8.	A	B	C	D	E
9.	A	B	C	D	E
10.	A	B	C	D	E
11.	A	B	C	D	E
12.	A	B	C	D	E
13.	A	B	C	D	E
14.	A	B	C	D	E
15.	A	B	C	D	E

Answers

Matching I—
Buildings A, B, C, D, E

On the mats provided, construct buildings A, B, C, D, E. Match each set of plans—BASE, FRONT, RIGHT—with the correct building.

NAME

Set 1

BASE (Front at Bottom)   FRONT   RIGHT   Matches building C

Set 2

BASE   FRONT   RIGHT   Matches building D

Set 3

BASE   FRONT   RIGHT   Matches building E

Set 4

BASE   FRONT   RIGHT   Matches building B

Set 5

BASE   FRONT   RIGHT   Matches building A

32   Worksheet 1-4

Developing Plans for Buildings

NAME

BASE

FRONT   BACK

RIGHT   LEFT

31

Worksheet 1-3

135

Answers

In each of these pictures is a mirror line. Everything on one side of the mirror will appear to be on the other side, too. Put in everything exactly as it would appear in the mirror.

34

On the mats provided, construct buildings AA, BB, CC, DD, EE. Match each set of plans—BASE, FRONT, RIGHT—with the correct building.

Set 1

BASE
(Front at Bottom)   FRONT   RIGHT

Matches building

BB

Set 2

BASE   FRONT   RIGHT

Matches building

EE

Set 3

BASE   FRONT   RIGHT

Matches building

DD

Set 4

BASE   FRONT   RIGHT

Matches building

AA

Set 5

BASE   FRONT   RIGHT

Matches building

CC

Worksheet 1-5

33

Answers

Drawing Plans

NAME

F.

BASE   FRONT   RIGHT

G.

BASE   FRONT   RIGHT

H.

BASE   FRONT   RIGHT

I.

BASE   FRONT   RIGHT

Worksheet 2-1   47

Through the Looking Glass

NAME

In these pictures you are shown part of what is on each side of the
mirror. Complete the picture so that each side is the mirror image
of the other.

Worksheet 1-7   35

137

Answers

Incomplete Plans

1. Create a building that has this BASE and RIGHT. Draw its FRONT. Record your building on a mat plan.

Numbers indicate height of columns.
There are 18 possibilities.

3141 (Illustrated)	2342	1141
3142	2341	2242
3241	1242	2241
3242	3341	2141
1342	3342	2142
1341	1142	1241

2. Create a building that has this BASE and FRONT. Draw its RIGHT. Record your building on a mat plan.

Number indicates height of columns.
There are 15 possibilities.

3322 (Illustrated)	3112	2321
3122	3222	2312
3321	3221	1322
3312	3212	1321
3121	2322	1312

3. Create a building that has this FRONT and RIGHT. Draw its BASE. Record your building on a mat plan.

X's indicate other possibilities

4. Create a building that has this FRONT and RIGHT. Draw its BASE. Record your building on a mat plan.

X's indicate other possibilities

Worksheet 2-2

48

Building from Plans

Use the plans to construct Buildings J–S. Use the BASE of each set of plans to make a mat plan record of your building.

J

K

L

M

N

O

P

*A 1 or 2 may be placed in each of the empty cells provided that each row and column marked with an asterisk has a 2 somewhere.

Q

R (non-standard base)

S

Worksheet 3-1

53

Answers

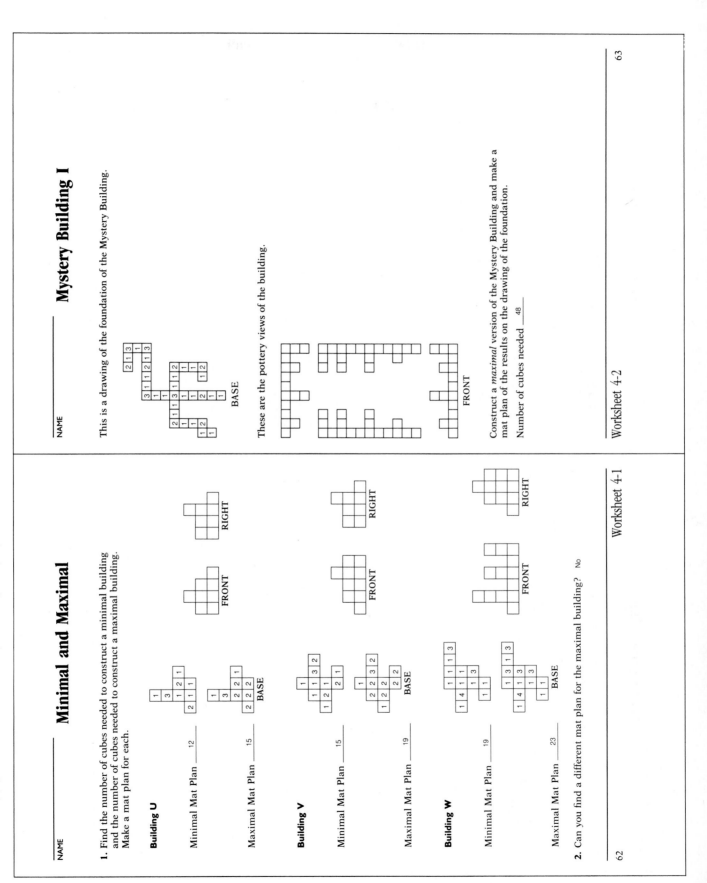

Minimal and Maximal

NAME _____

1. Find the number of cubes needed to construct a minimal building and the number of cubes needed to construct a maximal building. Make a mat plan for each.

Building U

Minimal Mat Plan ___12___

Maximal Mat Plan ___15___   BASE

FRONT   RIGHT

Building V

Minimal Mat Plan ___15___

Maximal Mat Plan ___19___   BASE

FRONT   RIGHT

Building W

Minimal Mat Plan ___19___

Maximal Mat Plan ___23___   BASE

FRONT   RIGHT

2. Can you find a different mat plan for the maximal building? No

Mystery Building I

NAME _____

This is a drawing of the foundation of the Mystery Building.

BASE

These are the pottery views of the building.

FRONT

Construct a *maximal* version of the Mystery Building and make a mat plan of the results on the drawing of the foundation.

Number of cubes needed ___48___

Answers

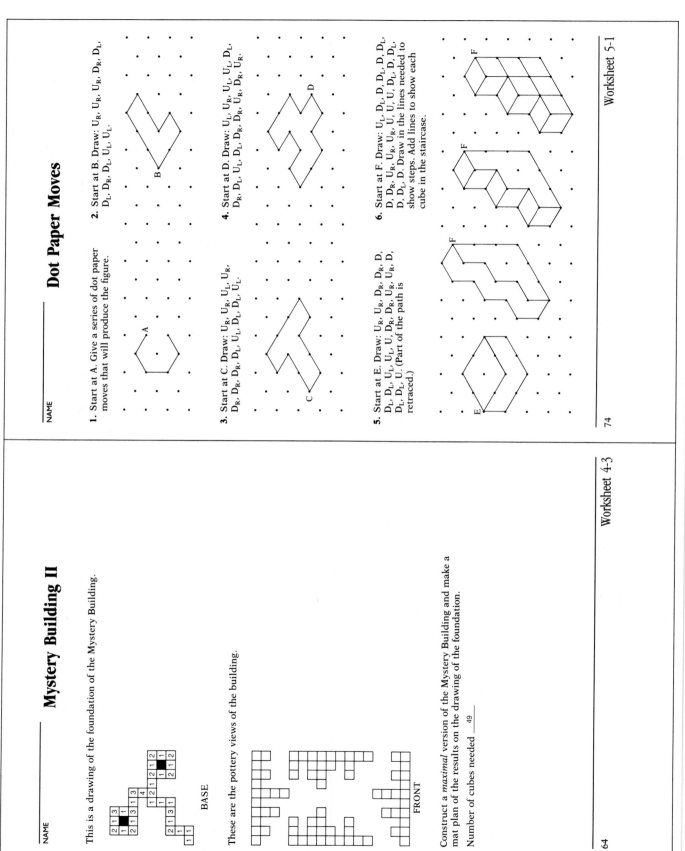

Dot Paper Moves

1. Start at A. Give a series of dot paper moves that will produce the figure.

A

2. Start at B. Draw: U_R, U_R, U_R, D_R, D_L, D_L, D_R, D_L, U_L, U_L.

B

3. Start at C. Draw: U_R, U_R, U_L, U_R, D_R, D_R, D_R, D_L, U_L, D_L, D_L, U_L.

C

4. Start at D. Draw: U_L, U_R, U_L, U_L, D_L, D_R, D_L, D_R, D_R, D_R, U_R.

D

5. Start at E. Draw: U_R, U_R, D_R, D_R, D_L, D_L, U_L, U_L, U_L, U_L, U_L, U_R, D_R, D_R, D_R, U_R, D_L, D_L, U_L, U_L, D_L, U_L. (Part of the path is retraced.)

E   F

6. Start at F. Draw: U_L, D_L, D_L, D, D_L, D, D_L, D, D_R, U_R, U_R, U_R, U, U, U_L, D_L, D, D_L, D, D_L, D. Draw in the lines needed to show steps. Add lines to show each cube in the staircase.

F

F

Worksheet 5-1

Mystery Building II

This is a drawing of the foundation of the Mystery Building.

BASE

These are the pottery views of the building.

FRONT

Construct a *maximal* version of the Mystery Building and make a mat plan of the results on the drawing of the foundation.
Number of cubes needed ___49___

Worksheet 4-3

Answers

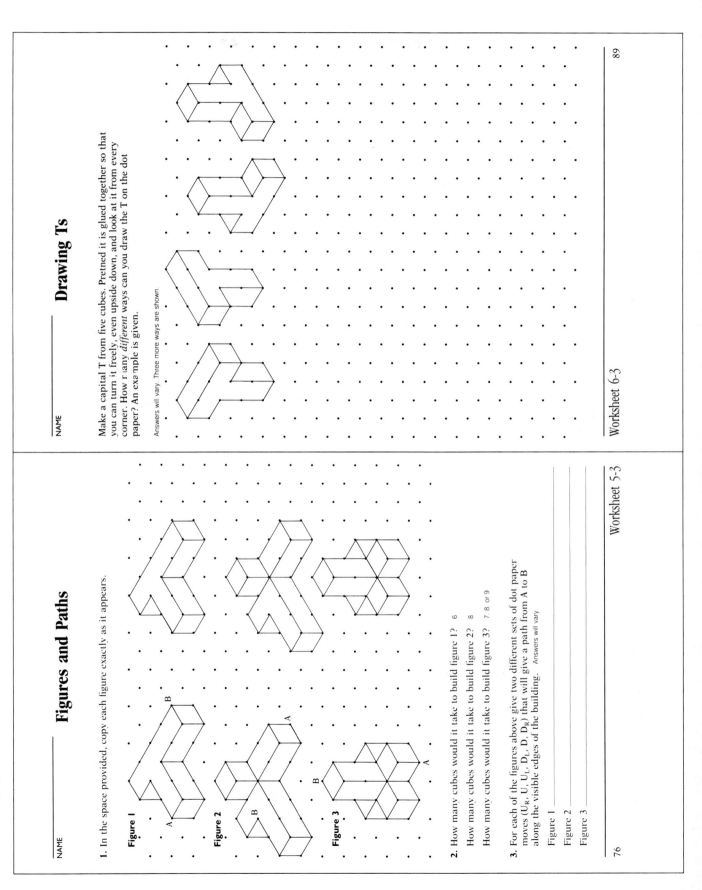

Figures and Paths

NAME _____

1. In the space provided, copy each figure exactly as it appears.

Figure 1

Figure 2

Figure 3

2. How many cubes would it take to build figure 1? 6

How many cubes would it take to build figure 2? 8

How many cubes would it take to build figure 3? 7, 8 or 9

3. For each of the figures above give two different sets of dot paper moves (U_R, U, U_L, D_L, D, D_R) that will give a path from A to B along the visible edges of the building. Answers will vary.

Figure 1 _____

Figure 2 _____

Figure 3 _____

Worksheet 5-3

Drawing Ts

NAME _____

Make a capital T from five cubes. Pretend it is glued together so that you can turn it freely, even upside down, and look at it from every corner. How many *different* ways can you draw the T on the dot paper? An example is given.

Answers will vary. Three more ways are shown.

Worksheet 6-3

Answers

Corner Views

Here are four views of building **BB**. Label the corner of the mat with the names of the visible sides of the building: FRONT, RIGHT, BACK, LEFT.

Do this part *after* you have completed Worksheet 7-2, Matching Isometric Views. Build and draw the four corner views of this building. Include a corner of the mat labeled with the names of the visible sides.

Worksheet 7-1   95

Matching Isometric Views

Build buildings AA, DD, and EE on the mat plans provided. Each of the buildings is drawn below from each of its corners. The corners are the FRONT LEFT, FRONT RIGHT, BACK LEFT, or BACK RIGHT. Match the building and its corner to the correct drawing. Indicate which corner the building is viewed from by writing in FRONT, RIGHT, BACK, or LEFT.

1. Building ___DD___

2. Building ___EE___

3. Building ___DD___

4. Building ___EE___

5. Building ___DD___

6. Building ___AA___

7. Building ___AA___

8. Building ___EE___

9. Building ___DD___

10. Building ___AA___

11. Building ___EE___

12. Building ___AA___

96   Worksheet 7-2

Answers

NAME

Adding and Removing Cubes

Build each building with cubes. Take away the shaded cube or cubes and draw what remains.

1.

2.

3.

Either or both of the dotted cubes could appear.

4.

5.

Build each building. Then add a cube to each shaded face and draw the new building.

6.

7.

8.

9.

97

NAME

Hidden Cubes

1. Find several different buildings that have this FRONT LEFT view. Make a mat plan for each one.

FRONT

LEFT

Possible mats:

2. Find minimal and maximal buildings that have this FRONT RIGHT view. Draw mat plans for each. (Check your orientation.)

RIGHT

FRONT

Possible mats:

Minimal   Maximal

104

143

Answers

Copyright © 1986 Addison-Wesley Publishing Company, Inc.

Uniqueness

In each problem below you are given two corner views of the same building. Build a building with these views. Draw a mat plan for a building that could have these views.

1.

LEFT
BACK
FRONT
LEFT

2.

BACK
RIGHT
FRONT
LEFT

	1	1	4
3	1	1	1
		1	
		3	1

Adding and Removing Cubes II

Build each building. Then add a cube to each shaded face and draw the new building.

1.

2.

3.

4.

If you try to remove the cubes in these buildings, the buildings will collapse. Pretend the remaining cubes are glued together and draw what is left when the shaded cubes are removed.

5.

6.

7.

8.

Answers

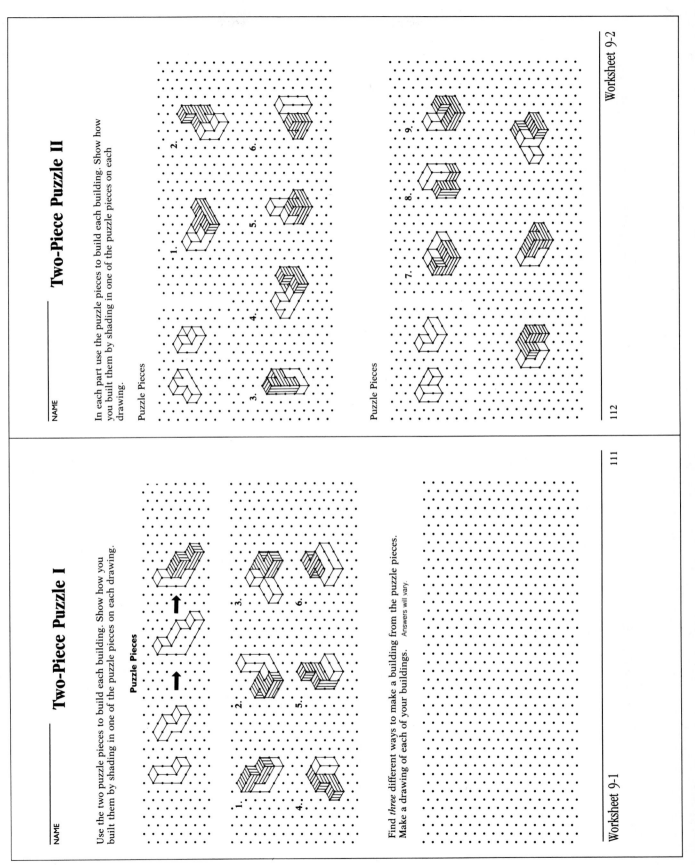

NAME

Two-Piece Puzzle I

Use the two puzzle pieces to build each building. Show how you built them by shading in one of the puzzle pieces on each drawing.

Puzzle Pieces

Find *three* different ways to make a building from the puzzle pieces. Make a drawing of each of your buildings. Answers will vary.

111

NAME

Two-Piece Puzzle II

In each part use the puzzle pieces to build each building. Show how you built them by shading in one of the puzzle pieces on each drawing.

Puzzle Pieces

Puzzle Pieces

Worksheet 9-2

Answers

Four Views

Build the following building and draw the view from each corner on isometric dot paper. Label each view by the corner from which it is drawn.

Building JJ

BACK			RIGHT
1	1		
		2	1
LEFT			FRONT

119

Drawing Single-Layer Buildings

Below is a mat plan for a building and an isometric drawing of the same building. It is the view of the building from the FRONT LEFT corner.

1			
1	1		
LEFT			FRONT

Each of these is a mat plan for a building. Build each building. Make an isometric drawing of the building as it looks from the FRONT LEFT corner.

Base 1

Base 2

Base 3

1.

2.

3.

Draw the buildings from another corner.

Answers will vary.

120

146

Answers

NAME _____

Eight Ways

You have learned different ways to draw a building and to give information about the building.

There is the architectural way, which draws views of a building from the FRONT, RIGHT and we could add, BACK and LEFT.

Then there is the isometric way, which can show a building from any of its four corners.

Here is a mat plan for a building KK.

BACK		
1	1	
2	1	3

LEFT / RIGHT / FRONT

Draw the four architectural views of the building and the four isometric views of the building.

Worksheet 10-3   121

NAME _____

The Archeologist's Explorations

An archeologist exploring a small isolated island has found the ruins of an ancient building. The mystery building had been made from large cubes of stone cut from the island quarry. The stones are scattered around the immediate area of the foundation of the building. The terrain and remoteness of the island suggest that no stones have been removed from the area.

There is a clear outline of the foundation of the building left in the ground.

Outline of the Base of the Archeologist's Mystery Building

122   Worksheet 10-4

147

Answers

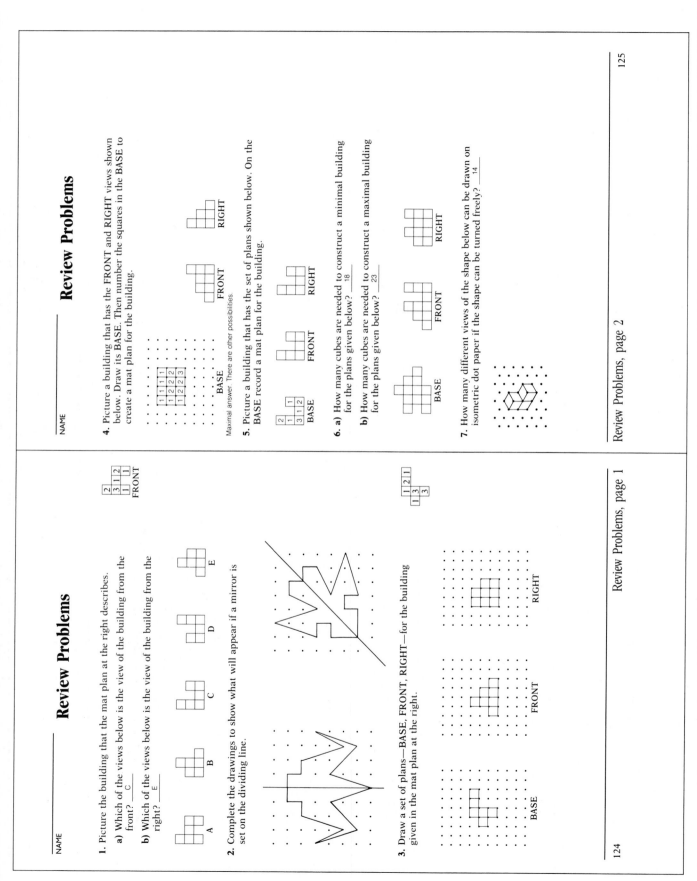

NAME

Review Problems

1. Picture the building that the mat plan at the right describes.

2		
3	1	2
1		1
FRONT

a) Which of the views below is the view of the building from the front? __C__

b) Which of the views below is the view of the building from the right? __E__

A   B   C   D   E

2. Complete the drawings to show what will appear if a mirror is set on the dividing line.

3. Draw a set of plans—BASE, FRONT, RIGHT—for the building given in the mat plan at the right.

1	2	1
1	3	
	3	

BASE

FRONT

RIGHT

Review Problems, page 1

NAME

Review Problems

4. Picture a building that has the FRONT and RIGHT views shown below. Draw its BASE. Then number the squares in the BASE to create a mat plan for the building.

1	1	1	1
1	2	2	2
1	2	2	3

BASE

FRONT

RIGHT

Maximal answer. There are other possibilities.

5. Picture a building that has the set of plans shown below. On the BASE record a mat plan for the building.

2		
1	1	
3	1	2

BASE

FRONT

RIGHT

6. a) How many cubes are needed to construct a minimal building for the plans given below? __18__

BASE

FRONT

RIGHT

b) How many cubes are needed to construct a maximal building for the plans given below? __23__

BASE

FRONT

RIGHT

7. How many different views of the shape below can be drawn on isometric dot paper if the shape can be turned freely? __14__

Review Problems, page 2

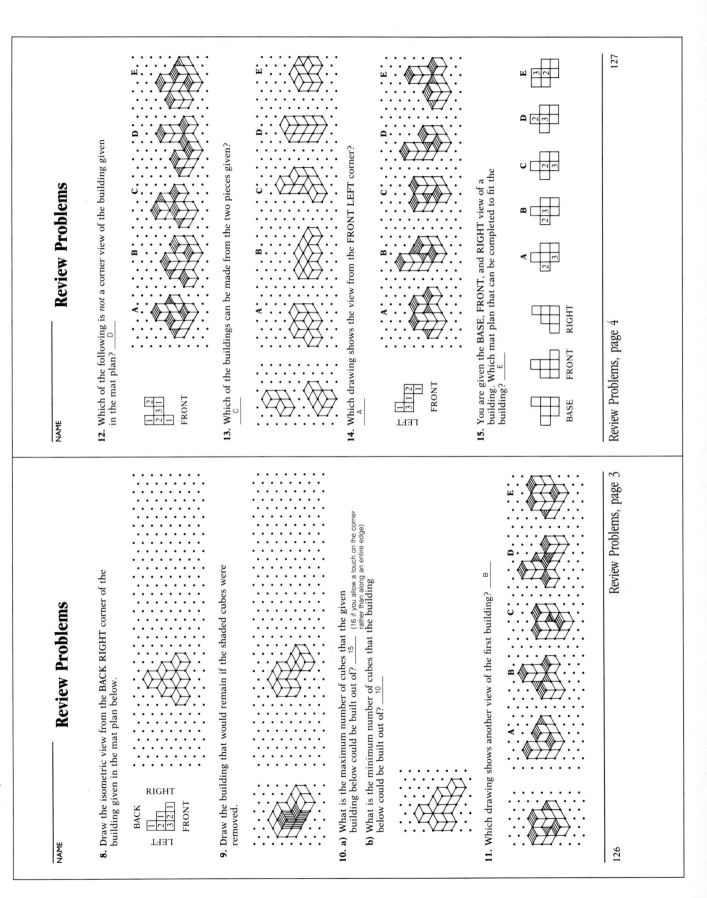

Review Problems

NAME

8. Draw the isometric view from the BACK RIGHT corner of the building given in the mat plan below.

9. Draw the building that would remain if the shaded cubes were removed.

10. a) What is the maximum number of cubes that the given building below could be built out of? 15 (16 if you allow a touch on the corner rather than along an entire edge)

b) What is the minimum number of cubes that the building below could be built out of? 10

11. Which drawing shows another view of the first building? B

126   Review Problems, page 3

Review Problems

NAME

12. Which of the following is *not* a corner view of the building given in the mat plan? D

13. Which of the buildings can be made from the two pieces given? C

14. Which drawing shows the view from the FRONT LEFT corner? A

15. You are given the BASE, FRONT, and RIGHT view of a building. Which mat plan that can be completed to fit the building? E

Review Problems, page 4   127

149

Unit Test Answer Key

Sample 1. D

Sample 2. A

1. D

2. B

3. A

4. E

5. D

6. B

7. D

8. B

9. E

10. B

11. D

12. D

13. E

14. D

15. C